AMERICAN IMMIGRATION

Volume 4

Citizenship and Naturalization – Employment Opportunities

GROLIER
EDUCATIONAL

First published in the United States in 1999 by Grolier Educational,
Sherman Turnpike, Danbury, CT 06816

When referencing this publication, use the following citation:
American Immigration. 10 volumes. Danbury, CT: Grolier Educational, 1999.

Photo Credits:
Pages 5, 8, 9, 11, 13, 14, 15, 18, 19, 20, 21, 22, 23, 26, 28, 29, 30, 32, 34, 35, 39, 40, 44, 45, 48, 49, 54, 63, 64, 67, 68, 69, 71, 73, 75, 79, 80, 82, 83, 84, 87: AP/Wide World Photographs
Pages 1, 43, 53, 62, 90: Courtesy Ellis Island Immigration Museum/NPS
Pages 56, 57: The Danish Immigrant Museum, An International Cultural Center

Oral histories provided by Ellis Island Museum Oral History Project/National Park Service

A Creative Media Applications, Inc. Production

Project Coordinator: Matt Levine

Writers: Michael Burgan, Robin Doak, Matt Kachur, Joanne Mattern

Editors: Dorothy Anderson, Barbara Jean DiMauro, Kathleen White

Design and Production: Alan Barnett, Inc.

Associated Press Photo Researcher: Yvette Reyes

Ellis Island Librarian: Barry Moreno

Ellis Island Volunteer: David H. Cassells

Director, Ellis Island Museum Oral History Project: Paul E. Sigrist Jr.

Oral History Transcribers: Nancy Vega, John Murieillo, Ann Bunley, Elysa Matsew, Roger Herz

Oral History Typist: Andrew Frisch

American immigration
            p.   cm.
      Summary: An alphabetical reference work examining the background,
statistics, reception, and current status of those groups who have immigrated
to America throughout history.
      ISBN 0-7172-9283-5 (set : hardcover : alk. paper). — ISBN 0-7172-9284-3
(v. 1 : hardcover : alk. paper). — ISBN 0-7172-9285-1 (v. 2 : hardcover : alk. paper). —
ISBN 0-7172-9286-X (v. 3 : hardcover : alk. paper)
      1. United States — Emigration and immigration — Juvenile literature —
Encyclopedias. [1. United States — Emigration and immigration — Encyclopedias.]
I. Grolier Educational Corporation.
JV6450.A59   1999
304.8'73 — dc21   99–18077
                                                                           CIP
                                                                            AC

Printed in the United States of America

Contents

PREFACE

Immigration has played an enormous role in the history of the United States. Numerous ethnic backgrounds have combined over the centuries of our country's existence, and in this modern time it is not unusual to find people who claim a variety of heritages yet still clearly think of themselves as American. Further, the contributions of other cultures to American society are countless. People in the United States are exposed every day to food, clothing, art, and language that have been strongly influenced by ideas from races and nations around the world.

In many ways the history of U.S. immigration tells the history of our country. This set explores U.S. immigration and tells the stories of those who have *emigrated,* or left their homelands, so they could *immigrate* to, or enter, the United States. All have come to America with one common goal: to better their lives in some manner in a new land.

The set has two introductory volumes—the first an overview of U.S. immigration, and the second a historical account of Ellis Island in New York, where millions of immigrants in the 19th and 20th centuries first set foot on American soil to be processed before they made their ways to their final destinations in this country. The volumes that follow are an encyclopedic reference on immigration topics and immigrant groups from A to Z. Entries about particular immigrant groups include locator maps. A dotted line on a map points to a specific country or continent from which an immigrant group has originated; a circle outlines a more general region from which an immigrant group has come. There are cross-references to related topics at the end of most entries in the box labeled *See also.* An icon of the Statue of Liberty appears with each *See also* box. Additionally, some main entry headings are followed only by cross-references to other entries (for example, ABOLITIONIST NEWSPAPERS— See LITERATURE, THE MEDIA, AND ETHNICITY). These cross-references direct readers to the entries containing the information they seek. (Cross-references are not used within the introductory volumes; the first two volumes have information that will naturally apply to all the entries in the A-to-Z volumes.) The set index, which is included at the back of each volume, also can help readers quickly find specific subjects within the set. A list of suggested further reading about immigration is provided as well for students to use for subsequent research.

To add to the richness of the subject matter, sidebars appear throughout the set, providing interesting facts and stories regarding immigrants and immigration. Transcripts of interviews from the Ellis Island Museum Oral History Project have also been included in the set. The interviews provide personal accounts of what it was like for those who chose to seek a new life in this country. The interviews are denoted by a ship icon to make them easy to locate. They were lightly edited for readability. Original language usage and spellings were retained in the numerous quotations cited throughout the set.

CITIZENSHIP AND NATURALIZATION

To enjoy the full political and legal benefits of living in America, immigrants must become United States citizens. By law, anyone born in the United States is a citizen, so in some cases children of immigrants might be citizens years before their parents become citizens, *if* the parents acquire citizenship at all. In some cases people born outside the country can live permanently in America without ever becoming citizens. Immigrants to the United States who have not become citizens are known as *aliens.*

Immigrants who choose to become citizens go through a process called *naturalization* and are referred to as *naturalized citizens.* Naturalized citizenship gives people full legal rights, although in the past Congress tried to pass laws taking away naturalized citizenship for certain legal offenses. The U.S. Supreme Court ruled that most of those laws were unconstitutional; only people who lie about their past or their intentions while going through the naturalization process can be stripped of their citizenship. Those offenders are also deported from of the country.

The Supreme Court, however, has upheld laws that strip both native-born and naturalized citizens of their citizenship. Americans can lose their citizenship for various reasons, including swearing *allegiance* (loyalty) to another country or becoming naturalized citizens of another country, serving in the military of another country without permission from the U.S. government, voting in foreign elections, spying for another country, and trying to overthrow the U.S. government by force. A person can also voluntarily give up American citizenship.

The American concept of citizenship has its roots in English laws. The English laws stressed a subject's loyalty to the monarch. In return, the monarch protected his or her subjects. Each party had responsibilities to the other. That relationship carried over to the American relationship between its citizens and their government.

Immigrants are sworn in as U.S. citizens in April 1917.

■ Colonial America

The English settlers who lived in the American colonies were British subjects. During the 17th and 18th centuries the English monarch (most often a king) and Parliament had the power to make British subjects of non-English immigrants who went to America. Many Europeans leaving for America, such as the French Huguenots, stopped in England to become naturalized British subjects before heading to the colonies. The colonial governments, however, always wanted more settlers, and colonies such as Virginia and New York encouraged immigrants by offering to naturalize settlers who immigrated to their colonies.

The English government ended the colonies' practice of naturalization in 1700, although it still allowed the colonies to grant a form of local citizenship that applied only within the colony granting the privilege. Parliament passed a naturalization law in 1740 that allowed immigrants to become British subjects while they were in America. The law required immigrants to live in a colony for seven years, with no more than two consecutive months spent outside the colony. The potential subject also had to swear allegiance to the king and an oath before the Christian God. Jews and Quakers were allowed to swear different religious oaths; Roman Catholics were not allowed to become naturalized subjects. Catholics were thought to be more loyal to the pope than to the crown. Naturalized immigrants had the same rights as native-born British subjects.

After 1763 the English government began to place more restraints on its American colonies, and that control applied to naturalization as well. In 1773 New Jersey and Pennsylvania passed naturalization laws for their colonies,

Today's Oath of Allegiance

Immigrants make the following oath to become naturalized citizens:

I hereby declare, on oath, that I absolutely and entirely renounce and abjure all allegiance and fidelity to any foreign prince, potentate, state, or sovereignty of whom or which I have heretofore been a subject or citizen; that I will support and defend the Constitution and laws of the United States of America against all enemies, foreign and domestic; that I will bear arms on behalf of the United States when required by the law; that I will perform noncombatant service in the Armed Forces of the United States when required by law; that I will perform work of national importance under civilian direction when required by law; and that I take this obligation freely without any mental reservation or purpose of evasion, so help me God.

and Parliament struck down those acts. Three years later, in the Declaration of Independence, the American patriots cited that attempt to clamp down on naturalization as one of their complaints against King George III and his "absolute tyranny" over the colonies.

■ Citizens in the New Nation

After winning the Revolutionary War (1775–1783), the newly independent Americans created their first strong national government. In 1787 leaders gathered to draft the U.S. Constitution. The Constitution said little specifically about citizenship, although it did imply that citizenship was automatic for anyone born in the United States. The document gave Congress the power to naturalize new citizens, but the members of the Constitutional Convention argued about when naturalized citizens should be allowed to hold public office. One committee recommended a three-year wait before a naturalized citizen could run for the House of Representatives. A delegate, however, said, "Citizenship for three years was not enough for ensuring that local knowledge which ought to be possessed by the Representative." The final document allowed naturalized citizens to run for the U.S. House of Representatives seven years after becoming citizens and for the Senate after nine years. No naturalized citizen, however, could become president or vice president.

In 1790 Congress passed the Naturalization Act, which allowed a free, *white* immigrant who had lived in the United States for two years to apply for citizenship. For many years that mention of race prevented Africans and

Asians from becoming naturalized citizens. (See "Citizenship for Nonwhites" below.)

Five years later Congress made major changes to the naturalization process. The new law required a five-year residency period, and immigrants had to declare their intention to become citizens three years before they applied for naturalization. At the time they gained citizenship, immigrants swore an oath to uphold the Constitution and renounce allegiance to any foreign country.

During the next few years tensions in Europe and political disputes in America led to a growing distrust of foreigners on the part of U.S. citizens. The result was the Alien and Sedition Acts of 1798. One part of the act lengthened the residency requirement for naturalization to 14 years. Another naturalization law in 1802 put the requirement back to five years. The 1802 law also specified that wives and children under 21 automatically became citizens along with their husbands or fathers.

The naturalization process in the early 19th century was relatively easy—too easy in the eyes of some Americans. In 1838 the *New York Daily Express* reported the trial of a German American who helped German immigrants become citizens. According to witnesses, "everything was done in a hurry—few questions were asked—and individuals [were] admitted to the rights and privileges of citizenship without duly examining their qualifications." Some people also complained that immigrants were illegally naturalized so they could vote for the politicians who helped them gain citizenship. In some cases Americans made money by charging immigrants huge sums to make the naturalization process "easier."

The strong anti-immigrant feelings that arose in the 1830s led some Americans to demand a longer residency requirement before aliens became citizens. The Know-Nothing Party, which was strongly anti-Irish and anti-Catholic, wanted a 21-year waiting period and said foreign-born citizens should not be allowed to hold political office. Those ideas, however, never became law, although Massachusetts briefly kept naturalized immigrants from voting or holding office for two years after they became citizens.

Dred Scott's Day in Court

Dred Scott was a Missouri slave who spent time with his master in free states—states that did not allow slavery. Under Missouri law a slave who spent time in free states or territories and then returned to Missouri could sue for his freedom. In 1846 Scott did so. He won his freedom in a state court, but his owner appealed. The case was complicated, and it dragged on for years until reaching the U.S. Supreme Court in 1857.

By that time the issue was a national controversy. It stirred the country's pro-slavery and antislavery forces. Justice Roger Taney wrote the decision in the case, which has been called one of the worst legal opinions in American history. Taney ruled that Scott was still a slave and that slaves were property and not citizens. Blacks in general, Taney said, had long been considered "beings of an inferior order" who did not have the same rights as whites. Free blacks might hold state citizenship, but they could not become U.S. citizens. Taney's harsh language helped fuel the feelings that led to the Civil War (1861–1865).

◼ Citizenship for Nonwhites

The Naturalization Act of 1790 was directed specifically at white immigrants, and the status of Native Americans and African Americans was largely ignored in the Constitution. For many years the U.S. government considered Native Americans citizens of their own tribal nations; they were not offered citizenship until 1924. The issue for African Americans was more complex.

As individual states abolished slavery, many let freed blacks become state citizens, which implied they also had national citizenship. The Constitution did not explain the difference between

state and national citizenship, although it said states had to honor the rights of citizens from other states. As tensions over slavery grew, Southern states passed laws forbidding free blacks to cross their borders; Southern lawmakers refused to recognize blacks' rights as citizens of other states. The issue of citizenship for blacks—slave or free—came to a head in 1857 in the Dred Scott case, which resulted in a decision that blacks could not be U.S. citizens. (See "Dred Scott's Day in Court" sidebar on page 3.)

Taking the Test

When applicants for naturalization go for their final papers, Immigration and Naturalization Service officials quiz them on their knowledge of American history and politics. Some questions are fairly easy, but others are more difficult. Here are a few sample questions from the test.

1. What are the colors of the flag?

2. How many states are there in the Union?

3. What are the three branches of our government?

4. Who said "Give me liberty or give me death"?

5. Who wrote "The Star-Spangled Banner"?

6. Who has the power to declare war?

Answers:

1. red, white, blue   2. 50   3. legislative, executive, judicial   4. Patrick Henry   5. Francis Scott Key   6. Congress

■ A New Era: The 14th Amendment and Beyond

In 1868 the United States adopted the 14th Amendment to the U.S. Constitution. The amendment overturned the Supreme Court ruling in the Dred Scott case and gave African Americans citizenship, granting it "to all persons born or naturalized in the United States" (although Native Americans and most Asians were still excluded). Two years later blacks who had been born in Africa were given the right to become naturalized citizens of the United States.

The 14th Amendment also guaranteed African Americans citizenship in the states in which they lived. The amendment said that no state could unjustly deny the "privileges and immunities" that came with U.S. citizenship.

The amendment was very important for many immigrants as well. The legal concepts of equal protection and due process, which guarantee equal rights and fair legal treatment, were granted to "any person," not just citizens. (The same wording was used in the Bill of Rights in 1788.) Many immigrants gained legal protection against unfair state and federal laws.

However, the citizenship status of Asian immigrants already in the United States or those who arrived after 1868 did not change. The Constitution gave Congress the power to set naturalization procedures, and those regulations still applied only to free, white people; Asians were not considered white. Among Asians only children of Asian ancestry *born* in the United States could become U.S. citizens. The legal discrimination against the Chinese in particular was strengthened in 1882, when Congress banned Chinese immigration.

■ Naturalization Act of 1906

The next major change in naturalization laws came in 1906. A law passed that year created the Bureau of Immigration and Naturalization, replacing the old Bureau of Immigration. The process for naturalization became more streamlined and uniform, with immigrants going through a three-step process to gain citizenship. (That basic procedure is still used today.)

Immigrants wanting to becoming citizens began by filing their "first papers," which indicated their desire to become naturalized. Next the applicants filed their "second papers," their formal request to become citizens. Then, during a 90-day period, naturalization officials investigated the immigrants' backgrounds. Public hearings were held to determine whether citizenship should be granted. Two witnesses had to swear to each applicant's good morals, and the immigrants had to answer questions about American history and politics and speak some English. (See "Taking the Test" sidebar.) When all the requirements had been met, the immigrants were granted U.S. citizenship.

■ Promoting and Limiting Naturalization

Around the time the new naturalization law was passed and through World War I (1914–1918), the United States went through another round of intense anti-immigrant feelings. At the same time that many people wanted to keep out new immigrants, the United States was making a push to "Americanize" the immigrants who were already in the

country. In 1910 more than half the foreign-born males in the country—almost 4 million—were aliens. That statistic was not kept for women until 1920; that year, more than half the foreign-born residents of both sexes were aliens. The government began to work with private organizations to encourage immigrants to become citizens and to educate applicants for citizenship about American values.

Not all immigrants, however, wanted to become U.S. citizens. Many planned to return to their homelands. Others were reluctant because of their treatment in America. One Italian, who waited 12 years before becoming naturalized, later wrote: "What had there been during the first three or four years of my residence in this country which would have made citizenship at all attractive to me?… Had I not been sneered at as an undesirable?"

Other immigrants who wanted to become naturalized were held back by the racial qualifications for citizenship. Dark-skinned people from Asia and people from Mexico who were

Vietnamese refugees take an English lesson, one step on the road to becoming naturalized citizens.

Caucasian were considered "non-whites" by the courts and were denied the right to become citizens. Some immigrants from the Middle East had to go to court to fight for their right to be naturalized, and some courts refused to let immigrants of mixed European and Asian background become U.S. citizens.

Marriage Penalty for Women

American women faced many legal hurdles in the early part of the 20th century, and their problems extended to citizenship concerns. A 1907 law said any woman born in the United States who married an alien acquired her husband's nationality and lost her U.S. citizenship. When a man born in the United States married a foreign-born woman, however, the woman became a U.S. citizen.

In 1915 Ethel Mackenzie challenged the law after she married a Scottish immigrant and California officials declared she was no longer a U.S. citizen. Mackenzie, who was born in the United States, took the matter to the U.S. Supreme Court. The Court agreed with California. "The identity of husband and wife," the Court said, "is an ancient principle … and this relation and unity may make it of public concern in many instances to merge their identity, and give dominance to the husband."

The unequal treatment remained in effect until 1922. From then on an American-born woman remained a citizen regardless of her husband's nationality—as long as he was eligible for naturalization—and a foreign-born wife of an American-born man had to apply for citizenship. However, until 1931 if a woman born in the United States married an alien ineligible for naturalization, she lost her citizenship.

During this period Congress passed other laws that restricted who could become naturalized or, in one case, that took away the citizenship of Americans who married aliens. (See "Marriage Penalty for Women" sidebar.) In 1917 Puerto Ricans officially became U.S. citizens, but the residents of another American territory—the Philippines—did not. After World War I a person's perceived loyalty to the United States during the war could affect naturalization status. Foreign-born pacifists and others who had opposed the war were not allowed to become naturalized.

■ World War II and After

Right before World War II (1939–1945) Congress again made changes to the naturalization laws. A 1940 law allowed native people of Alaska to become citizens. Three years later Chinese immigrants were finally allowed to become naturalized, although the ban on other Asians remained. Filipinos and Native Americans were given the right to naturalize in 1946. The biggest changes came a few years later, with the Immigration and Naturalization Act of 1952.

■ The McCarran-Walter Act

The Immigration and Naturalization Act of 1952 is usually known as the McCarran–Walter Act, after its two sponsors: Senator Patrick McCarran of Nevada and Representative Francis Walter of Pennsylvania. McCarran was the chair of the Senate committee that studied the entire system of immigration laws. The McCarran–Walter Act finally ended all racial restrictions on naturalization as well as restrictions based on sex and marital status.

The law also added a new requirement for naturalization: the ability to read and write English as well as the ability to speak some English. Aliens were required to register each year with the federal government. The act made it easier for the U.S. government to deport aliens, and more categories of deportable people were created. Aliens who were drug addicts, who belonged to groups that opposed the U.S. government, or who were connected with immoral practices could be deported.

The McCarran-Walter Act was the last major change to U.S. naturalization laws. Since that law was passed, immigration to the United States has reached record levels and so has the number of naturalized citizens. In the 1960s more than 114,000 immigrants were naturalized during the entire decade; in 1996 alone about 1.6 million resident aliens applied for citizenship and slightly more than 1 million were naturalized. By 1997 the country had more than 9 million naturalized citizens out of a foreign-born population of almost 26 million.

Ellis Island Museum Oral History Project

NAME: Sister Mary Hilarine Tesar
COUNTRY: Austria
YEAR IMMIGRATED: 1914
AGE: 14 years
INTERVIEWER: Paul E. Sigrist Jr.

SIGRIST: Talk to me about how your father learned how to speak English, if he did indeed learn how.

TESAR: My father learned how to speak English from me. In school we had … a bilingual school from grades one to six. We learned Czech and English one hour each day, Czech to English, English to Czech. So and we had sisters who knew the language. Up to grades seven, seven and eight…. And so that was very wonderful, because then I could learn. I used to carry a dictionary under my arm. And when I heard a word … used, and I didn't know what it was, I looked it up. And I

learned a lot. So then at home my father wanted to get his citizenship papers. So he had a book too. He had to answer certain questions, as today you have to study your citizenship book. So he would say, "Mary, what's this? Please show me. What's this? What's that?" [She gestures.] So I had to learn how to use a dictionary and helped him out in English. And he did his first papers. Yes. The second papers he got when I was in the convent already. And that time was dangerous, because they said if you didn't have your second papers, you would have to be sent back to … the country you came from. So I wrote to my father for … just before my birthday, it was. And I said, "Please, Papa, get your citizenship papers." And he did.

Where Do Naturalized Citizens Come From?

The chart below shows Immigration and Naturalization Service figures for the top ten countries from which citizens naturalized in 1996 came.

Country	Number of People Naturalized
Mexico	217,418
Cuba	62,168
Vietnam	47,625
Philippines	45,210
Soviet Union	36,265
El Salvador	33,240
China	30,656
India	28,932
Dominican Republic	27,293
Colombia	26,115

SOURCE: U.S. Immigration and Naturalization Service

He was already working on it. And on my birthday he got his citizenship papers. Yeah.

SEE ALSO: Assimilation; Immigration Law and Policy; Intermarriage; Literacy; Prejudice and Discrimination; Race

CRIME

In the 1800s and early 1900s making a new life in the United States was not always easy for immigrants. Many who arrived from distant shores—especially those who settled in America's big cities—were ill prepared. Besides having to adjust to a new culture, most immigrants found themselves living in neighborhoods that were poor, overcrowded, and potentially dangerous. As more and more immigrants crowded into America's cities, the rates of poverty, alcoholism, violence, and crime increased sharply.

As the first wave of immigrants flooded into the United States in the early 1800s, a pattern began that repeated itself over the next decades. A series of different ethnic groups, beginning with the Irish, monopolized illegal markets and crime. After one group *assimilated* (adopted American ways) and moved upward and out of the slums, a new immigrant group took its place, both in the tenement neighborhoods and as the leader in crime and black markets.

▌ Targets of Crime

From the moment immigrants set foot in the United States, they were targeted by con artists, criminals, and others hoping to take advantage of the newcomers' low social status as well as any language barriers that might exist. In the early and mid-1800s dishonest boardinghouse keepers paid men called "runners" to meet ships of immigrants arriving in ports. The runners targeted immigrants who arrived with no friends or relatives awaiting them. With no one to guide them to a reputable boardinghouse, the immigrants were easy marks.

A runner would round up immigrants, sometimes taking their luggage right out of their hands. The runner would then lead the immigrants to a boardinghouse, where the boardinghouse keeper would grossly overcharge them. If the immigrants did not have the means to pay for their lodging, the boardinghouse keeper might keep their possessions as payment.

Immigrants traveling from New York City to destinations farther west were also targets of scams. Dishonest ticket agents used false scales when weighing luggage and even forced immigrants to

Charles "Lucky" Luciano (center), a notorious leader of organized crime, was arrested in 1936 and later deported to his homeland of Italy.

purchase tickets twice—once in New York City and a second time in Albany, which was a stopping-off point for all trips west.

Mean Streets and the Rise of Gangs

Between 1820 and 1850 more than 42 percent of all people entering the United States were Irish, fleeing a life of poverty and famine in the old country. Most of them had little or no money and were forced to settle in the major port cities where they landed. Such cities as New York, Philadelphia, and Boston saw their Irish populations increase sharply during the 1840s and 1850s. By 1860 one of four New Yorkers was Irish-born.

The poor, squalid tenement neighborhoods, nicknamed "Irish Towns" or "Shanty Towns," became hot spots for criminal activities. In New York City the Bloody Third, the Bloody Ould (Old) Sixth, and Hell's Kitchen were just three neighborhoods that earned reputations for high levels of fighting and crime. In the mean streets of such areas, thugs randomly beat and robbed passersby. Victims, usually other immigrants, rarely reported such attacks to the police. Language barriers, cultural attitudes, and mistrust of the police were some reasons victims did not report the crimes.

Irish immigrants were the first group to form criminal gangs in the United States. In the 1800s such gangs as the Forty Thieves, the Short-Tail Gang, the Dead Rabbits, and the Plug Uglies roamed an area of New York's Lower East Side called Five Points. Five Points was one of the most infamous neighborhoods anywhere. Charles Dickens, who visited Five Points in

1842, described it as "reeking everywhere with dirt and filth . . . debauchery has made the very houses prematurely old."

However, only a small number of Irish immigrants chose a life of crime. In Five Points, as in other neighborhoods, honest immigrants trying to get by in the New World lived in tenements near brothels, saloons, and alleyways where gangs met. Unfortunately, the Irish as a whole were subject to prejudice and discrimination precisely because of the abject conditions and high crime rates that existed in some of their neighborhoods. An article in the *Chicago Post* stated: "The Irish fill our prisons, our poor houses. . . . Scratch a convict or pauper, and the chances are that you tickle the skin of an Irish Catholic. Putting them on a boat and sending them home would end crime in this country."

In the late 1800s, as many of the earlier Irish immigrants assimilated and became successful, they moved out of the inner-city neighborhoods. New groups of immigrants arriving in the

Officials stand in front of a load of alcohol captured at the Mexico-Texas border during Prohibition.

United States began to replace the Irish in the poorest of tenement neighborhoods. Soon two of those immigrant groups—Jews and Italians—replaced the Irish as the most notorious criminals.

By the early 1900s New York's leading gangsters were either Irish, Italian, or Jewish. Then came an event that completely changed the face of crime in the United States. In January 1920 the 18th Amendment, banning the making and the sale of alcoholic beverages, was enacted. Prohibition had begun, and the stage was set for the first national organized crime syndicate.

Don Vito: The Father of the American Mafia

Before Lucky Luciano, Meyer Lansky, and Al Capone there was Don Vito Cascio Ferro, an Italian immigrant and the man believed to have established the Mafia in America.

In 1893 Ferro fled to the United States after being accused of a number of crimes, including kidnapping, extortion, and arson. After arriving in New York, Ferro formed a group called the Black Hand. Members of the Sicilian Mafia traditionally sent a picture of a black hand to the rich as an unspoken demand for money.

The members of the Black Hand were mostly criminals who, like Ferro, had fled Sicily to escape arrest. Once in the United States, the group picked up where they had left off in Italy, extorting money from shop owners and others in exchange for "protection."

Ferro was forced to leave New York when police began investigating his connection to the brutal murder of a rival. He settled in New Orleans, established a counterfeiting ring, and arranged for the smuggling of heroin from Sicily. Ferro eventually returned to Sicily, where he became the head of the Mafia there. In 1929 the "Boss of Bosses" was imprisoned on false charges of murder by Fascist leader Benito Mussolini. He remained in jail until his death in 1945.

■ Prohibition and the Mafia

Prohibition, called America's "noble experiment," did not quench people's desire to drink. The demand for alcohol was strong, and illegal saloons called *speakeasies* sprang up across the nation. *Bootlegging,* the illegal production and transportation of alcohol, became a thriving business. Criminals saw the opportunity to become rich and quickly stepped in to fill the void. Sicilian groups in particular dominated the black market, illegally providing alcohol for a large profit.

Mafia groups had been operating in several U.S. cities since the late 1800s. (See "Don Vito" sidebar.) But Charles "Lucky" Luciano, a Sicilian immigrant who arrived in the United States in 1906, was the person who organized the groups, or "families," into one national crime syndicate. During Prohibition in the late 1920s Luciano sought the help of Jewish gangsters Meyer Lansky and Benjamin "Bugsy" Siegel to carry out his plan for a single, powerful Mafia organization. Those who opposed Luciano's plans were killed. Another famous Prohibition-era gangster was Al Capone, who dominated Chicago's bootlegging industry. Although Prohibition ended in 1932, the Mafia continued to thrive, concentrating its efforts on gambling, the drug trade, and other illegal activities.

■ Tongs: Chinese Organized Crime

In 1882 the Chinese Exclusion Act suspended Chinese immigration for ten years. Thousands of Chinese men, too poor to return home, were stranded in the United States without their families. By 1890 there were an estimated 27 Chinese men to every Chinese woman.

The immigrants banded together in neighborhoods dubbed "Chinatowns." The first and most famous Chinatown was in San Francisco, California. The population consisted mainly of male Chinese immigrants who had been separated—sometimes permanently—from their families by strict immigration laws aimed specifically at the Chinese. People fell into poverty and despair, and the neighborhood soon became a center of violence and illegal activity as well. Brothels, gambling halls, and opium dens attracted Chinese and whites alike.

The groups in control of the illegal activities were the *tongs,* secret societies of Chinese immigrants. Tongs originated in ancient China to oppose brutal warlords. As immigrants made their way to America, so did the tongs.

Each tong had a certain territory; when one tong infringed upon the territory of another, violence was likely. In the 1920s "tong wars" made the newspapers and alarmed San Francisco officials, so much so that in 1933 the U.S. government deported a large number of tong members.

As immigration restrictions eased in the 1930s and 1940s, the nature of the tongs began to change. Many tong members opened restaurants and shops to attract a growing tourist trade to Chinatowns, completely ending all their criminal activities. Others dropped the name *tong,* choosing instead titles such as "merchant association." Today tongs still exist throughout the United States. Some are merely Chinese-American community organizations; others, however, are ganglike and engage in illegal activities.

■ Immigrants and Crime Today

Recent law enforcement efforts have considerably weakened the Mafia in the United States. However, new criminal elements have stepped in to fill the void. Mobsters from Russia, Hong Kong, Jamaica, Mexico, and other places cause problems in the United States. The major activity of the new breed of

immigrant criminals is illegally smuggling and selling drugs such as cocaine and heroin.

Another growing illegal activity involves smuggling people from China and other countries into the United States. That trade is extremely profitable: people from China may pay up to $50,000 per person to reach this country. Very few can afford that kind of fee in advance; they may pay part up front, then, after arriving in the United States, work for the smugglers until the balance is paid. Although some may be required to work in restaurants and sweatshops, others might be forced to beg, deal drugs, or become prostitutes.

As in earlier times, the majority of immigrants entering the United States, both legally and illegally, are honest people looking for a better life. However, the few immigrant criminals

Meyer Lansky is arrested on drug charges in Miami, Florida, in 1970. Lansky, along with fellow gangsters Charles "Lucky" Luciano and Benjamin "Bugsy" Siegel, organized a national crime syndicate that came to be known as the Mafia.

continue to give their ethnic groups bad reputations and provide fuel for anti-immigrant opinions.

SEE ALSO: Chinese; Illegal Immigrants; Irish; Italians

CROATS

The Republic of Croatia, a boomerang-shaped nation slightly smaller than West Virginia, is located in south-central Europe. Ethnic Croatians, who are mostly Roman Catholic, make up 78 percent of the nation's population; about 12 percent are Orthodox Serbs.

Immigrants from Croatia began arriving in the United States in the 17th century. The first group of immigrants intermarried and *assimilated* into (adapted to) U.S. society, but later groups of Croatian immigrants were more successful at maintaining their Croatian culture and ethnicity in their new land. Croats are one of the largest Slavic ethnic groups in the United States.

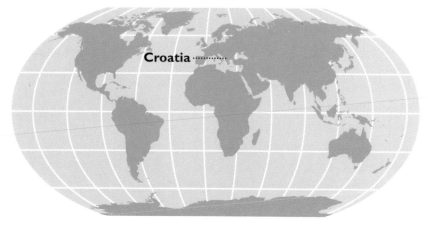

Croatia

■ History

In the 5th, 6th, and 7th centuries the area now called Croatia was settled by Croats, a Slavic people. Croatia became a kingdom in the 10th century. In 1091 it was conquered by Hungary, which in turn was conquered by the Austrian Hapsburgs in the late 17th century. In 1867 the Dual Monarchy of Austria-Hungary was created, and Croatia remained a part of the Austro-Hungarian Empire until the end of World War I (1914–1918).

In 1918, after Austria-Hungary's defeat in World War I, Croatia joined with Serbia, Slovenia, Bosnia and Herzegovina, and Montenegro to form the Kingdom of the Serbs, Croats, and Slovenes (later called Yugoslavia). The Serbs repressed and discriminated against the Croats, and Croat resentment grew. In 1934 King Alexander of Serbia was *assassinated* (murdered, often for political reasons) by Croatian separatists.

During World War II (1939–1945) the Nazis set up a Fascist puppet government in Croatia, called the Independent State of Croatia. Leaders of that government expelled and killed thousands of Serbs, Jews, and Gypsies. In 1945 Croatia became part of Communist Yugoslavia.

In 1991, following the fall of communism, Croatia seceded from Yugoslavia, becoming the Republic of Croatia. Croatian Serbs took up arms, with the assistance of the Yugoslav military, and set up their own territory, the Republic of Serbian Krajina. However, all Serb territory reverted to Croatian control in 1995.

■ Coming to America

The first Croatian immigrants to the United States were a small number of sailors, merchants, and missionaries who arrived in the 17th and 18th centuries. They settled along the Gulf of Mexico, in such places as Louisiana, Alabama,

Mississippi, and Florida. As trade between the United States and the Dalmatian region of Croatia increased in the early 1800s, immigration also increased.

Like immigrants from other parts of the world, many Croatian immigrants were drawn to the West Coast during the California gold rush of the late 1840s and early 1850s. After the gold rush many stayed and worked in the copper and coal mining industries. By 1860 there were 20,000 Croats from the Dalmatian region living in the United States.

The greatest wave of immigration from Croatia occurred between 1880 and 1914. Beginning in the 1880s Croatian population centers in the United States changed as immigrants started settling in the East and the Midwest. Many Croatians made their homes in Pennsylvania; by 1908 about 85,000 Croats lived there, and their numbers continued to increase. Most of those arriving were unskilled laborers who took jobs in Pennsylvania's steel mills, iron foundries, and coal mines. Croatian immigrants also took jobs building roadways and railroads. Other highly industrialized areas—such as Chicago, Cleveland, and Detroit—also attracted Croats. Croatian immigrants worked in the mines and ore fields across the nation, including the silver mines of Nevada, the coal mines of New Mexico, and the copper fields of Michigan. In the late 18th century Croats controlled the oyster harvesting business near New Orleans. In pre–World War I San Francisco a group of Croats started an apple orchard. They developed new ways of preventing crop diseases and new ways of packing, drying, and shipping apples. Croatian

immigrant Stephen N. Mitrovich started the U.S. fig industry in California.

Early Croatian immigrants often identified themselves as Austrians, Bosnians, Dalmatians, Istrians, Magyars, Slovenians, or Venetians and weren't counted as a separate group by the Immigration and Naturalization Service until 1918. However, according to some estimates, from 1880 to 1914 about 500,000 people left Croatia and most of them immigrated to the United States. The peak year of Croatian immigration was 1907, when more than 80,000 immigrants entered the United States.

Most Croats left their homeland to escape poor economic conditions, which included a poor harvest, food shortages, and the decline of the industries—wooden-ship building, fishing, and wine making—that had sustained many Croatian workers. Most of those who immigrated to the United States were young men, sent abroad by their families to earn money. They wanted to save enough money to return to their homeland to pay off family debts and build homes. Between 1899

Bosnian Croats protest a 1995 Bosnian peace agreement that has made it impossible for them to return to their homes.

and 1924 about half of all Croatian immigrants returned home for some period of time.

In 1924 unlimited immigration of Croats came to a halt when U.S. immigration quotas limited Yugoslavia to fewer than 1,000 immigrants per year. Immigration quotas remained in effect until 1955, causing many Croats to migrate to Canada, Australia, and South America. In the 1940s and 1950s the Communist revolution in Yugoslavia drove thousands of Croats from their country. The immigrants were allowed into the United States as political refugees, and they were generally better educated than were previous immigrants from Croatia. From the late 1940s until 1990, about 70,000 Croats journeyed to the United States.

Ivan Grbac (left), the father of Kansas City Chiefs quarterback Elvis Grbac, shares traditional Croatian food and drink with others at a tailgate party before a Chiefs game in 1997.

■ Life in America

Life in the United States was not easy for early Croatian immigrants, especially those who were unskilled or semi-skilled. Croatian fraternal organizations helped immigrants by providing them with health and life insurance as well as

death benefits. The first national Croatian organization, the Croatian Union, was founded in 1894 in Allegheny City, Pennsylvania. In its earliest days the Croatian Union protected about 600 members. Ten years later it claimed more than 22,000 members in 281 lodges nationwide. The union was not the only Croatian fraternal organization. By 1912 about 1,500 Croatian fraternal organizations were active throughout the United States.

Other important institutions for Croatian immigrants included saloons and boardinghouses. The saloons served as ethnic centers where immigrants could meet with those who spoke the same language and shared the same culture. At saloons immigrants could hear the latest news from their homeland and receive financial and legal advice from the saloon keepers. Saloon keepers also acted as intermediaries and interpreters for the immigrants and the Americans with whom they interacted.

The boardinghouses were kinds of cooperative households set up to give male Croatian immigrants places to eat and sleep. Ten or more boarders, usually from the same Croatian village or district, might live in a boardinghouse. Some boardinghouses were run by Croatian women; others were run by male "bosses," who cooked and cleaned. At other boardinghouses, boarders divided the chores and responsibilities among themselves.

During the earliest years of Croatian immigration few women came to the United States. Most male Croat immigrants who stayed married women of other ethnicities, including Irish, Mexican, and Spanish. Most of those early immigrants found maintaining their cultural traditions difficult, as most of their children identified with the nationality of the mother.

Beginning in the 1930s, however, many more Croatian women began to immigrate to the United States. That brought about an increase in organized ethnic activities, including an increase in the number of Croatian Roman Catholic parishes. As Croatian families set up neighborhoods in the United States, they found it easier to preserve ethnicity. In fact, many Croatian women learned only enough English to get by in the new land.

Even though immigrant children attended public schools and learned English, the Croatian tradition of strong extended-family ties encouraged Croats to continue living in ethnic neighborhoods. After World War II new immigrants from Croatia also settled in the established ethnic communities, helping to keep Croatian culture alive. Croatian-language newspapers, publications, and folklore groups also helped.

According to the 1990 Census, 544,000 Americans reported Croatian ancestry. Forty-three percent of those people lived in the Midwest, although Pennsylvania has a larger Croat population than any other state.

Croatian Americans have a strong sense of Croatian nationalism and cultural identity. The Croatian World Congress, for example, is a group for Croatians living outside Croatia that has branches everywhere Croats live. The group publishes brochures, newspapers, and periodicals and sponsors many educational and public-relations activities.

The Croatian Union still exists today, although it is now known as the Croatian Fraternal Union. With 100,000 members, it is the largest organization of Croats outside Croatia. The group's stated goal is to preserve Croatian culture and identity in America.

Famous Croatian Americans include Croatian-born inventor Nikola Tesla, who developed the alternating current (AC) system of power and held more than 700 patents; violinist Zlatko Balokovic; famous sculptor Ivan Mestrovic; Mike Stepovich, governor of the Alaska Territory in 1957 and the state's first governor in 1959; and Rudy Perpich, governor of Minnesota in the late 1970s.

SEE ALSO: Bosnians; Hungarians; Serbs; Slovenes

Putting aside the traditional animosity between their two countries, a Croatian and a Serb play basketball in 1995 for Rutgers University's men's basketball team in Piscataway, New Jersey.

CUBANS

Among recent immigrants to the United States—those who arrived within the last 30 to 40 years—perhaps no group, with the exception of Russian

Jews, has been driven to emigrate because of politics more than Cubans. Many immigrants from all groups often plan, at least initially, to return to their homeland once they've achieved a certain level of economic stability. Early Cuban immigrants, fleeing the Communist government of Fidel Castro, identified themselves as political exiles with no plans to remain permanently in the United States. They did not leave their homeland by choice but were forced out by a hostile political government. Many of those Cuban immigrants insisted, and still insist, that once Cuba is rid of Castro, they will return home to reclaim their rightful place in Cuban society.

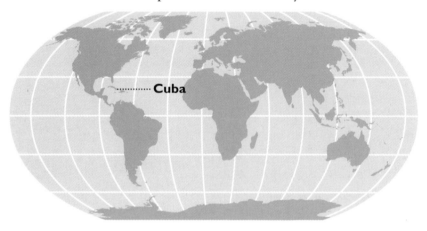

More recent Cuban immigrants, however, were driven less by political concerns and more by economic ones. As Castro's reign stretched into its fourth decade, more and more Cuban immigrants came to identify the United States as their home and made no plans to return to Cuba, even if Castro was removed from office and a democratic system of government established. However, several factors ensure that interest in the Cuban homeland will not soon disappear: the poor political and economic relationship between the United States and Cuba, the closeness of Cuba to the United States (Cuba is an island nation just 90 miles off the southern tip of Florida), and the still fervent hopes of the first generation of Cuban immigrants that someday they'll be able to return home.

History

Originally inhabited by native tribes, Cuba was colonized by the Spanish in 1511. The Spanish introduced disease, warfare, and a policy of enslavement that wiped out the native population. The island was seized by the British in 1762. The British encouraged the cultivation of sugarcane (subsequently Cuba's major industry), which flourished under the care of African slaves. The sugar industry continued under the direction of the Spanish, who regained control of Cuba within a year.

The horrible conditions of slavery, along with resentment of colonial domination by Spain, fueled independence movements in Cuba throughout the 19th century. In the early 1890s José Martí, while living in exile in New York, led the effort to free Cuba from Spanish control. U.S. troops intervened on Cuba's behalf and defeated Spain in the Spanish-American War (1898). The United States ruled Cuba for four years before turning control over to a succession of right-wing dictators, who did little to alleviate the sufferings of Cuba's poor people. (See "José Martí" sidebar.)

The reign of right-wing dictators finally came to an end in 1959, when Fidel Castro succeeded in overthrowing Fulgencio Batista. Castro quickly became an enemy of the United States by proclaiming a socialist state and installing himself as its leader for life. Castro's Communist ideology directly threatened the lifestyles of Cuban industrialists and other wealthy people who had made their fortunes under Batista and his predecessors. Immediately after the 1959 revolution those people became the first to flee Cuba.

Castro sought support from the Soviet Union, at the time the world's preeminent Communist country. (The Soviet Union collapsed in 1991 when many of its republics declared independence.) Fearing a Communist outpost just 90 miles from the United States, U.S. leaders immediately cut off diplomatic relations with Cuba and shortly thereafter imposed a complete economic *embargo* (a ban on importing or exporting goods) aimed at forcing Castro from power. Even after the fall of communism in the Soviet Union and Cuba's loss of Soviet economic support, the U.S. embargo has done little to displace Castro.

■ Coming to America

Prior to the 1959 Cuban revolution, few Cubans immigrated to the United States. In the early 1800s some Cubans lived in southern Florida, where they worked on tobacco plantations. In the late 19th and early 20th centuries more substantial numbers of Cubans immigrated to the United States to escape the hardships of Cuba's struggle for independence from Spain. A significant number of those immigrants used the United States as a base from which to agitate for and plan Cuba's battle for independence.

A small number of Cubans immigrated to the United States in the early 1950s to escape the oppression of the Batista regime. The vast majority of modern-day Cuban immigration, however, followed Castro's revolution in

1959. The first Cuban immigrants at that time were Batista supporters and other land-owning and middle-class Cubans whose way of life was threatened by Castro's policies. Between 1959 and 1962 nearly 155,000 people left Cuba for the United States. They and subsequent immigrants were granted easy entry into the United States as a means of demonstrating America's hostility toward Castro. In 1962 commercial air traffic between the two countries was suspended and not resumed until 1965. Between 1965 and 1972 more than 257,000 Cubans left Cuba for the United States by means of daily flights from Varadero, Cuba, to Miami, Florida. That "airlift" was halted in 1973.

José Martí

The most famous Cuban poet, patriot, and martyr of the 19th century, José Martí became a symbol of Cuba's struggle for independence from Spain. Throughout colonial Central America and South America, Martí's name was synonymous with liberty.

Martí was born in 1853. He was educated in Havana, Cuba. As an adult he was jailed more than once for his public support of revolutionary movements. He was exiled first to Spain, then to Venezuela, and finally to New York City, where he lived from 1881 to 1898. While in exile, he earned a law degree, wrote poetry, and published political essays. An officer of the Cuban Revolutionary Party from 1892, Martí planned an invasion and the liberation of Cuba. He died in Cuba in 1898 while fighting for the cause to which he had dedicated his life. Radio Martí, a U.S.-supported effort to transmit uncensored news reports into Communist Cuba, is named for this Cuban hero.

In 1980 Castro allowed Cubans living in the United States to visit Cuba. The impression the "rich cousins" made on Cubans produced a demand for emigration that Castro could not ignore. He allowed nearly 125,000 people to leave the island, traveling to the United States on homemade rafts available to them. Many sail from Cuba in homemade boats, braving the rough waters that separate the United States and Cuba. The earliest of the recent Cuban immigrants were driven by political conditions and were mostly middle class and well-to-do, but later immigrants came to the United States because of dire economic need.

Cuban immigrants to the United States settled for the most part in southern Florida. They created a lively community known as "Little Havana" in an area of Miami that had been mostly vacant and undeveloped land. Little Havana today forms a bustling center of Cuban-American culture. Cuban-owned businesses, including restaurants, bakeries, theaters, banks, and pharmacies provide services to the Cuban community. Little Havana in particular and Miami and southern Florida in general mark the obvious center of Cuban immigration to the United States.

Through a plan in effect from 1961 to 1981, the U. S. government sought to disperse the Cuban population more evenly throughout the United States. The sudden entry of large numbers of people who needed help strained the ability of the Miami city government to supply that help. Most of the Cubans resettled by that program ended up in New York and New Jersey, but a large number returned to the Miami area in the late 1970s and early 1980s. Los Angeles has the third largest population of Cubans after Florida, New York, and New Jersey.

and in leaky boats. The exodus came to be known as the Mariel boat lift, after the port from which the immigrants left Cuba. United States officials suspected that Castro shipped numerous criminals and psychiatric patients to the United States. Because of that suspicion and the poverty of the immigrants, many were treated harshly after arrival in the United States.

Since the Mariel boat lift a steady stream of Cuban immigrants has arrived in the United States by any means

A group of Cuban refugees land at the Key West Naval Base, Florida.

■ Life in America

Cuban Americans' opposition to the Castro regime characterized their early years of political activity in the United States. As Cuban immigrants became

more settled in the United States, their interests broadened to include local politics. They helped elect Cuban members of Congress, mayors and, in 1987, the first Hispanic governor of Florida, Bob Martinez. As a group Cuban Americans vote in higher percentages than do other Americans. Although not as well-off, on average, as native-born Americans, Cuban Americans enjoy the highest standard of living among Hispanic Americans. Cuban Americans also tend to be well educated and to have a very high literacy rate.

For the most part, Cuban immigrants enjoyed a warm reception in America because of strong anti-Castro and anti-Communist sentiments in the country during the 1960s. However, as opposition to Castro waned and the Communist threat to America vastly diminished, attitudes toward more recent Cuban immigrants changed. The poor immigrants are seen as economic burdens rather than as effective political symbols in the fight against communism. The opposition to Castro splintered around the question of America's contribution to the plight of the people in Cuba. Many, including Pope John Paul II, said that America's refusal to trade with Cuba hurts the Cuban people, not Castro. (See "The Pope Travels to Cuba" sidebar.)

Overall, Cuban Americans are perceived to be one of America's most vibrant and successful immigrant groups. Given their large and concentrated populations and their continued use of Spanish from one generation to the next, Cuban immigrants have experienced few difficulties in maintaining their culture in the United States. Cuban and American societies share many interests, particularly baseball. The influx of talented baseball players—such as Livan Hernandez, World Series MVP for the 1997 Florida Marlins baseball team—has had a major impact on America's "national pastime."

Other Cuban Americans have made significant contributions in entertainment (Desi Arnaz, Andy Garcia, Gloria Estefan); in business (Roberto Goizueta, CEO of Coca Cola); in literature (Oscar Hijuelos); and in politics (Ileana Ros-Lehtinen, the first Hispanic woman elected to the U.S. Congress).

Signs in both English and Spanish are typical of Miami neighborhoods where Cuban refugees have settled.

SEE ALSO: Political Participation; Spanish

CULTURAL CONTRIBUTIONS

The population of the United States consists almost entirely of immigrants, whether they arrived very early or just last week. Therefore, the culture of the United States is actually a combination of *all* immigrant cultures, brought by people who arrived from many parts of the world and then changed under the influence of American life. Cultural contributions, of course, extend far beyond the arts. The many different perspectives and experiences of various ethnic groups of immigrants contribute to American culture and enrich all Americans' lives. The arts are, however, a good indicator of the comprehensive immigrant influence.

The New Orleans Madri Gras, a festival traditionally held in Paris, is an example of French culture in the United States.

Unlike many parts of the world, especially countries in Europe and Asia, the United States has no continuous cultural traditions that have developed in the same place for centuries. The culture has always been carried by immigrants from other settings, then combined with elements borrowed from different immigrant cultures to create something that has never existed in exactly that way before. Alexis de Tocqueville, a French political thinker, visited America in 1831. A few years

later, he wrote that American society "comprises all the nations of the world … people differing from one another in language, in beliefs, in opinions; in a word a society possessing no roots, no memories, no prejudices, no routine, no common ideas, no national character." Tocqueville seemed to suggest that Americans were starting over and creating a society that had never existed in the Old World. That sense of creating something new is part of America's culture.

One way that new cultural forms and styles developed was through the combination of old and new. Immigrants naturally wanted to hold on to the traditions and art forms they had grown up with. At the same time they wanted to become Americans, and that often meant adopting a new language and new ways of expressing themselves. Artists, writers, actors, composers, and filmmakers looked for ways to build on what they had learned in their home countries. For many, the goal was to modernize and "Americanize" the old traditions while keeping their important elements alive. Those people's success in blending old and new made American culture incredibly diverse and exciting.

However, the development of the culture of late 20th-century America did not always happen smoothly. Often people whose immigrant ancestors had arrived early in the country's history had come to think of themselves as the "real" Americans, and they saw later arrivals as strange and uncivilized in every way. People often considered the newest immigrants "dirty." The American writer Gertrude Stein wrote sarcastically about that in 1934 in a book called *The Making of Americans:*

"The French tell me it's the Italians who never do any washing, the French and the Italians both find the Spanish a little short in their washing, the English find all the world lax in this business of washing, and the East finds all the West a pig, which is never clean.... And so it goes." As time went on, however, newer arrivals found their places in the established society and eventually became "older" groups themselves. They proceeded to look down on the cultural traditions that still later groups were bringing to America.

In the meantime, sometimes in spite of themselves, people who were already in America were influenced by the ideas and art forms expressed by people in each new group. The borrowing and blending of every aspect of culture, from the instruments people played to the kinds of jokes they told, created a mixture of styles and viewpoints that formed the mosaic of American culture.

■ Fine Arts (Painting and Sculpture)

Until about 1800, American art followed the European traditions that the early immigrants knew. Most paintings of the time were portraits of wealthy people who could afford to pay an artist to paint their pictures or landscapes painted in the European style. Artists of that time came from England, Germany, Holland, Sweden, Denmark, France, and Switzerland. Many immigrant artists, along with American-born artists, traveled to the great cultural centers of Europe to study art and to see the European masterpieces. They returned to America to create their own masterpieces, which reflected what they had seen and learned.

By the early 1800s more artists had arrived from Europe, especially from Italy, Russia, and the Scandinavian countries. They too followed the traditions of their own cultures, but they painted a wider variety of subjects.

For example, John Lewis Krimmel, who immigrated to the United States from Germany in 1810, began painting scenes of ordinary people in their everyday lives, and other artists followed his lead. In 1819 John James Audubon, who grew up in Haiti and France, started creating watercolors of birds. Eventually he made 435 paintings, which were published between 1827 and 1838 under the title *Birds of North America*.

French, English, and Italian sculptors also came to the United States, where they created many of the well-known sculptures in Washington, D.C. Their works greatly influenced American artists who had never seen the monumental sculptures of European cities.

As the frontier moved westward in the mid-1800s, immigrant artists as well as native-born artists became fascinated with

The Detroit Afro-American Festival, complete with traditional music, art, and food, is an example of Kenyan culture in the United States.

the majestic landscapes of endless plains, towering mountains, and wild, rushing rivers. Dramatic paintings of the western landscapes by a German immigrant, Albert Bierstadt, in the 1860s helped

Costumed Hispanic participants in New York City's Loisaida Street Carnival gather annually to welcome the summer with food, music, and dancing.

make that kind of picture popular.

Meanwhile, *folk art*—work by untrained artists that is generally simpler and less formal than fine art—had always been a part of Americans' lives. Joshua Johnston, a freed slave who came from the West Indies, was the first black professional artist in America; he painted portraits in the early 1800s and influenced later folk artists, both blacks and whites.

Traditional European styles in painting and sculpture continued to influence American art through the 19th century, as American artists traveled to Europe to study and European artists immigrated to America. In the early 1900s new ideas, mainly from France, caused tremendous excitement, as well as shock and horror, in America. New styles, including impressionism and cubism, rejected the old realistic art forms and presented a

vision of the world from each artist's unique point of view. American painters and sculptors who had worked in Europe subscribed to such revolutionary ideas, and European immigrants became part of the art centers in New York and other cities.

Modern communications and travel have made it easy for artistic influences to flow back and forth around the world in the 20th century. Marc Chagall, though not an immigrant, lived and worked in the United States for many years. His Russian-Jewish-French background played an important role in the development of his dreamlike works, which opened the eyes of many American artists. The powerful social commentary of Ben Shahn, who came from Lithuania, was influenced by the political and artistic ideas of the Mexican muralist Diego Rivera when both men lived in New York. Black artists, such as Romare Bearden, combined modern European styles with African images to create strong designs. Arshile Gorky, who immigrated to the United States from Armenia, was influenced by European and South American surrealists. His work in turn influenced a whole generation of 20th-century American artists, such as Jackson Pollock and Willem de Kooning.

Visual arts, such as painting and sculpture, cross borders more easily than do arts that depend on written or spoken language. The history of visual art in America reflects a combination of innumerable cultural traditions, ideas, and means of expression.

▌ Literature

Until the second half of the 19th century influences on literature in America came mainly from immigrants from English-speaking countries. That isn't surprising. Literature depends on the skillful use of language; poetry is difficult to translate successfully, and relatively few novels were written in any language before 1800. But beginning in the late 1800s, immigrants of all ethnic backgrounds began to write, and publishers began to publish, books about the immigrant experience.

Some American writers welcomed the arrival of immigrants and their varied cultures and ideas. Ralph Waldo Emerson wrote enthusiastically, "The energy of Irish, Germans, Swedes, Poles, and Cossacks, and all the European tribes,—and of the Africans, and of the Polynesians,—will construct a new race, a new religion, a new state, a new literature.…" Other people feared that America's culture, even its identity, would be destroyed.

Immigrants wanted to write literature that would tell the truth, as they saw it, about their lives. They wanted to counteract the demeaning stereotypes that often appeared in popular songs and traveling shows. And they wanted to explain their backgrounds and their traditions in ways that would encourage other Americans to accept them and not see them as strange. An example is Norwegian immigrant Ole Rölvaag's novel *Giants of the Earth,* written in 1927, about his immigrant community in South Dakota.

Such literature by immigrants had a strong influence on writings by people who were born in America. Perhaps the best-known is Willa Cather, who was not an immigrant but wrote about immigrants' experiences. Her 1918 novel *My Antonia,* about Bohemian (or Czech) immigrants in Nebraska, became very popular and is still read today. As interest in realistic fiction grew, others wrote about their own ethnic communities. William Saroyan's stories about Armenian-American life in Fresno, California, were widely read in the mid-20th century.

The novel *Yekl, A Tale of the Ghetto,* which is about Jewish life in New York City, was written by Russian immigrant Abraham Cahan in 1896 and was read by many people all over the United States. From it and other works by Jewish authors began a strong tradition of Jewish writing in America. Humorous books and serious books supplied a picture of Jewish life in the United States. Some important and popular names in 20th-century Jewish-American literature are Herman Wouk, Chaim Potok, Saul Bellow, Norman

Hungarian-born publisher Joseph Pulitzer came to the United States in 1864. He acquired the World, *the paper that set the style for today's newspapers.*

Mailer, and Philip Roth.

Other immigrants contributed to the development of Jewish literature. Sholom Aleichem came to America from Ukraine in 1906. His stories and plays about Jewish life in the old country were written in Yiddish, an everyday language used by many Jews throughout the world. They were very popular and were translated into English; in fact, they were the inspiration for the successful musical *Fiddler on the Roof* in the 1960s. (See "The Jewish Mark Twain" sidebar.)

A later immigrant from Poland, Isaac Bashevis Singer, wrote stories in Yiddish about Jewish life in Poland *and* in New York. His work, which won the Nobel Prize in literature in 1978, has helped keep Yiddish alive. Translated into English, his dreamlike tales and Eastern European Jewish humor have influenced many American writers.

After World War II (1939–1945) the experimental writer Vladimir Nabokov, born in Russia, and the Polish immigrant Jerzy Kosinski were important influences on American authors. American literature has benefited tremendously from the work of immigrant writers and their descendants, whose heritage includes the themes and styles of other cultures. Many immigrant writers wrote stories and novels about their fellow immigrants or about the life they had left behind. Recent works by Asian Americans such as Maxine Hong Kingston and Amy Tan have provided new examples of writing about immigrant communities.

◼ Movies

Compared with other art forms, movies are quite new; Thomas Edison held the first public viewing of a motion picture in the United States in 1896. Movies caught on quickly, especially after sound was added to the moving picture around 1927. In Europe as well as in the United States audiences were excited about this amazing innovation in the arts. Some of the most important people in American movies were immigrants. Samuel Goldwyn, for example, was a Polish immigrant who became one of the most powerful producers in Hollywood. Stars like Greta Garbo, from Sweden, set the style for a certain type of movie actress—sophisticated, mysterious, and European.

In the 1920s European filmmakers, especially in Germany and Russia, were experimenting with movie techniques. For example, some used dramatic contrasts of light and shadow to express characters' inner feelings. American movie companies invited European directors and actors to make films in Hollywood, and their influence was soon felt in American movies. For instance, the powerful realism of films by Erich von Stroheim, an Austrian immigrant who was an actor and a director, was widely admired and imitated. Ernst Lubitsch, born in Germany, came to the United States in 1924 and began making films in a very different style—witty, sophisticated comedies that influenced many makers of similar films.

During the 1930s many European filmmakers fled to the United States as Adolf Hitler rose to power. Some, such as Fritz Lang from Germany and Jean Renoir of France, made important films that affected many people's understanding of events in other parts of the world. Lang's first American film was *Fury*. Made in 1936, *Fury* is a powerful story of a small town taken over by an angry lynch mob. The movie reflects the political chaos that led so many Germans to flee the policies of the Third Reich. In 1945 Renoir's *The Southerners* dramatized the plight of

The Jewish Mark Twain

Soon after Sholom Aleichem (the name means "peace be with you") arrived in New York in 1906, he appeared with Mark Twain at a lecture hall. Aleichem was introduced to the audience as the "Jewish Mark Twain." Twain delighted Aleichem when he responded, "I am the American Sholom Aleichem."

poor farmers struggling to keep their land. At the same time, small growers all over Europe faced the devastation of their farmlands during World War II. Alfred Hitchcock, who came from Great Britain to the United States in 1939, set the standard for American mystery and thriller movies. His methods of creating unbearable suspense are studied and imitated more than half a century later. (See "An Englishman in Hollywood" sidebar.)

After World War II European filmmakers continued to experiment with new subjects and innovative styles. Symbolism and images from dreams, stories driven by the psychology of the characters, and abstract themes with no plot lines or characters were just a few of the techniques experimental filmmakers used. During the 1960s such "art films" began appearing in U.S. movie theaters, and audiences found them exciting and thought-provoking. Soon some European filmmakers working in the new *genre* (form or style) immigrated to America, drawn by new audiences and the possibilities of American financing. Roman Polanski, from Poland, and Milos Forman, from Czechoslovakia (now two countries: The Czech Republic and Slovakia), brought an Eastern European *aesthetic* (ideas about art) to Hollywood. In 1975 Forman won an Academy Award for directing *One Flew over the Cuckoo's Nest*.

At the end of the 20th century American moviemakers incorporate the influences of films and filmmakers from Asia, Africa, South America, the Middle East, Australia, and Europe. American movies are seen all over the world; motion pictures have truly become an international art form.

■ Music

Immigrants brought the music of their cultures with them when they came to colonial America. They kept their songs and the wordless music alive by singing and playing together; they also heard the music of other ethnic groups and began to imitate the elements that pleased them. African music played and sung by slaves was especially important in influencing the popular music of the period.

An Englishman in Hollywood

Looking back on his decision to immigrate to America, Alfred Hitchcock felt he had made a wise choice. In England, he said, "the art of filmmaking was often held in contempt by the intellectuals.... No well-bred English person would be seen going into a cinema; it simply wasn't done." Hitchcock appreciated American audiences' enthusiasm for his clever, gripping thrillers, and he enjoyed the respect American filmmakers had for his work.

European classical music was also played in colonial America, often by immigrant performers; many music teachers were European immigrants. By the first half of the 19th century Americans were composing classical pieces based primarily on the European music they had learned; that music is still played today.

Popular music from 1800 to 1850 continued to combine elements from various immigrant cultures. Folk music evolved as it was passed along through families and within communities. It might have used rhythms from African music and a melody from an Irish song, with new words that reflected life in America. Religious music was changing too, setting old words to new melodies and chants. In 1805 an Italian immigrant, Lorenzo da Ponte, popularized Italian opera in the United

States, which had a major influence on later operettas and musical theater.

In the second half of the 19th century music seemed to be everywhere. Cities were big enough to support orchestras and opera groups, and bands played at picnics and parades. German immigrants especially were prominent members of orchestras, and Irish musicians often joined bands. Pianos were popular—any family who could afford one had one—and many immigrants were able to earn a living teaching proper young ladies to play popular songs. Irish melodies influenced composers of American popular songs. Music in theaters and dance halls reflected many influences, particularly that of African-American music, which itself had been influenced by other ethnic musical styles.

Jazz artists Louis Armstrong and Billie Holiday are shown in a still from the 1941 film New Orleans.

With all that variety, at the beginning of the 20th century the United States still did not have a unified musical tradition. Jazz, which combined distinctive African rhythms with other musical elements, including blues and dance music, was an exciting new sound. The growth of the recording industry made jazz available all over the United States and then all over the world. Opera and classical music were still written almost entirely by Europeans, but the Irish immigrant Victor Herbert achieved great success with his operettas, including *Babes in Toyland* and *Naughty Marietta,* which paved the way for a unique American theatrical form—the musical comedy. Russian immigrant Irving Berlin had a huge hit in 1911 with his song "Alexander's Ragtime Band."

After World War I (1914–1918) many immigrants made important contributions to American music. Austrian Arnold Schoenberg, Hungarian Béla Bartók, and German Paul Hindemith were leading composers of modern classical music. The theater music of German Kurt Weill had lasting influence. *The Threepenny Opera* showed how jazz could be combined with popular music for the stage, and *Down in the Valley* offered new interpretations of the songs of the Appalachian region of the United States.

In the second half of the 20th century additional ethnic musical traditions have energized American music. The Latin and Cuban sounds of Xavier Cugat earned a wide following; Hawaiian music based on Polynesian instruments has influenced many popular musicians and singers. American rock music grew out of a blend of several types of black music and white music, including blues, rhythm and blues, gospel, country and western, and the music of popular harmony groups, such as barbershop quartets. The earliest British rock musicians freely borrowed playing styles and tunes from American rockers. Both groups later shared an interest in the music and instruments of India and incorporated those influences into their work. The music of the Cajuns, descendants of French-Canadian immigrants to Louisiana, led to *zydeco,* which blends elements from Cajun, African-American, blues, jazz, and rhythm and blues traditions. *Conjunto* music in Texas combines the accordion and the polka dance sounds of German, Polish, and Czech immigrants with Mexican music. *Klezmer* music, a popular music in Yiddish-speaking communities in Poland, Romania, and Ukraine, has a growing appeal for audiences and musicians alike.

American music combines elements of many musical cultures; its vibrancy and excitement result from the unique mix of musical styles and traditions that immigrants introduced to the United States. Such contributions have helped create a diverse and flexible musical culture.

◼ Radio and Television

Radio reached the height of its popularity in the United States between 1930 and 1945. During the Great Depression of the 1930s radio broadcasts helped keep people cheerful. The device itself was inexpensive enough so that many homes could have one, receiving programming was free, and the idea that people all over the country were listening to the same show at the same time seemed to pull Americans together in a difficult time.

Many early radio shows were similar in some ways to the variety shows of the late 19th century; they included musical numbers and humorous dialogues or monologues as well as interviews and other features. Other popular radio shows were soap operas, comical family serials, and adventure series. Jewish humor influenced the radio tradition; one popular radio show, which later became a television success, was *The Goldbergs.* Early minstrel shows were also popular, and they led to such well-loved programs as *Amos and Andy.*

Opera: Italian and American

The composer Gian-Carlo Menotti came to America from Italy in 1928. He was trained in Italian opera and determined to adapt the traditions of opera to the cultural environment of America. He became the most successful American composer of opera of his time, and his opera *Amahl and the Night Visitors,* a retelling of the story of the Magi's gifts to the Christ child, is seen on television and presented in theaters throughout the country at Christmastime.

As television broadcasts began to reach more parts of the country in the late 1940s and early 1950s, radio shows lost much of their audience. Early television programming resembled radio; there were variety shows, family comedies, adventure series, and lots of comedy. Many of television's most popular comic stars were Jewish, and they brought a Jewish style of humor, influenced by immigrants, to their material. Another ethnic culture was glimpsed on the hugely popular show *I Love Lucy,* starring Lucille Ball; Lucy's husband, Ricky Ricardo, was played by the real-life Cuban bandleader Desi Arnaz.

Although most radio and television performers were not immigrants, their shows reflected the same ethnic influences that played roles in other aspects of American culture, such as literature, music, and theater.

Theater

Theater building began in the United States quite early; by the 1820s, for instance, Cincinnati, Ohio, already boasted two theaters. In addition to presenting plays, theaters also staged poetry readings and other literary events. Variety shows and minstrel shows remained popular until after the Civil War (1861–1865). Variety shows were made up of a number of acts that didn't usually have anything in common. Performers might sing, dance, tell jokes, do magic tricks or acrobatics, or demonstrate special talents, such as rope twirling or ventriloquism. White actors in blackface makeup performed minstrel shows; besides singing and dancing, they

Béla Lugosi, who immigrated from Hungary to the United States in 1921, became famous for his portrayal of Count Dracula, the vampire.

featured "black" dialect jokes and skits and music that used African-derived instruments—banjos, bones, and tambourines. Although many parts of the minstrel show were based on African forms and styles, much of the humor was patterned on Irish comedy and song shows of that time.

European immigrants appeared in minstrel shows as well as in regular plays. English actors and producers came to America to work in the theater. There was a French theater in New Orleans and a German one in New York. After the Civil War theatrical stars immigrated to the United States from such countries as England, Germany, and Ireland. Plays and operettas also "immigrated"; humorous operettas such as those by England's Gilbert and Sullivan found huge audiences in America.

American vaudeville began in New York City in 1881. The term *vaudeville* originated in France. Essentially, vaudeville was similar to the earlier variety shows, consisting of a series of singing, dancing, and other kinds of performances. However, in the late 1800s and early 1900s many vaudeville performers from England and France toured in America, and their sophisticated acts influenced American performers. The "varieties" became more elaborate and more ambitious in scale.

By 1900 other ethnic groups had begun to arrive in the United States. Jewish jokes and Jewish comedians began to appear on the stage, and their style of humor influenced both performers and playwrights. The 1920s saw an explosion of plays produced in New York City on Broadway and in other cities around the country. Some were German and British dramas whose new realism and focus on social problems influenced American playwrights greatly. Musicals too began to express more complex ideas than before.

Theater in the 20th century in America is affected by the ideas and cultural and political changes that occur in other countries. Playwrights and plays travel all over the world, and their innovations are adapted and modified differently in each country. Productions from Asia and Africa spur the emergence of ethnic theater in many American cities and influence the structure of new plays.

The history of theater in the United States is one of incorporating elements from many cultures and using them in innovative ways. Immigrants to America from many parts of the world have contributed to the American theater as producers, directors, actors, designers, and builders. Their skills and theatrical traditions have had an enormous influence on the development of the American theater.

Ellis Island Museum Oral History Project

NAME: Louise Wehrli Owen
COUNTRY: Switzerland
YEAR IMMIGRATED: 1923
AGE: 3 years
INTERVIEWER: Janet Levine

LEVINE: Do you remember any customs that your mother and father kept that maybe were Swiss and that they retained in this country?

OWEN: Oh, yes. Oh, things like canning foods, you know. And my mother's cooking; she was a very good cook. She had cooked for both Italian and Swiss families, and she knew a lot, and French. So she knew a lot of ways, and she was a great one to make us eat spinach pancakes, which she learned in a French home ..., and they were good.

LEVINE: Are there any other dishes that were Swiss that you recall?

OWEN: Oh, yeah. My mother made Swiss onion pie. She made *knopfle,* which is ... sort of like a ... dumpling that they have here. They were called knopfle.... I never called them dumplings. [She laughs.] Of course, being the only Swiss one, you know, the only one that was in Switzerland, I spoke a lot of words, and I remember when I started school it was not too difficult, because I didn't start till I was six, and I played with the children that lived around, and I learned the language quite well. That I do recall. And I remember I'd like to talk, and ... the first day I was in the school I had to sit in the corner, ... a dunce stool, like they usually have you do? [She laughs.] Like they did years ago? I remember that, and I cried because I didn't know why she put me there; it was just because I was talking while she was talking.

King Gustav VI of Sweden (left) presents the 1963 Nobel Prize in physics to Eugene P. Wigner on December 10, 1963. Wigner, a professor at Princeton University, was born in Hungary.

CULTURAL PLURALISM

Americans have often debated the best way to combine new immigrants into American culture, just as they have debated what that culture is and what it should be. In the past the dominant white Protestant majority, with its ethnic roots in Great Britain, often argued that its "Anglo" (English-influenced) culture was the one American culture and that new immigrants had to adapt to it. The adaptation process is called *assimilation*—an individual's or a group's accepting and adapting to another group's culture. Other people have argued that the Anglos and other immigrants have created a new, distinct American culture, as people from different races, religions, and ethnic groups have combined in a

Members of the Kerala Dance Theatre perform an Indian dance at the 1997 Lotus Festival. The festival is designed to bring together Asian and Pacific Island groups in a cultural exchange featuring ethnic dancing, music, martial arts, drama, and food.

"melting pot." The third major theory of how the different ethnic groups have—or should—interact is called *cultural pluralism*.

Cultural pluralism is the idea that immigrants from different ethnic groups retain their own culture in America, even as they become American citizens and adopt some of the attitudes and customs of the dominant Anglo culture. Proponents of cultural pluralism say that, to some degree, it has happened naturally. In a sense by becoming immigrants, people cut themselves off from their homelands and their identities. Preserving their cultures in America reestablishes some of those old ties. And once in America, it makes sense for immigrants to live in cities or neighborhoods with others from their homeland, to keep speaking their native language, and to follow old customs. Such ties to the old ways give a sense of security while the immigrants adapt to life in America.

Over time cultural pluralism has also become a deliberate goal of many ethnic, racial, and religious groups. The groups want to distinguish themselves from the Anglo culture that many white Protestant English Americans once assumed was the American culture. Cultural pluralism, especially in the latter half of the 20th century, has stirred pride among ethnic groups that might have felt trampled on by Anglo America.

■ The Birth of Cultural Pluralism

The formal concept of cultural pluralism was developed in the 20th century. (See "The Father of Cultural Pluralism" sidebar.) Until then most Americans accepted assimilation as the best way to create an American culture. Some writers and thinkers, however, had already recognized that the United States had distinct cultural groups, usually formed along racial, ethnic, or religious lines. President John Adams referred to the country as "a wonderful mix of nations," and poet Walt Whitman described America as "a nation of nations." To Alexis de Tocqueville, however, the mix was not always so positive. Tocqueville, a French aristocrat who studied the United States in the 1830s, believed the country had an uneasy blend of three races—white European, black, and Native-American. "Fortune has brought them together on the same soil," he wrote, "where, although they are mixed … each race fulfills its destiny apart." Racism in America has sometimes created a forced cultural pluralism, or separation of groups, which has socially and politically hurt the subjects of racial hatred. The positive cultural pluralism of the 20th century has helped ease some of that pain.

African Americans and Native Americans faced unique restrictions on their abilities to keep their cultures alive in the United States. Most European immigrants, however, had opportunities to re-create their cultures in America. They organized private schools where their children learned in depth about their own religions and spoke in their native languages. Immigrants attended religious services in their own tongues. And they could keep informed on events in their homelands and in their cultural communities in America by reading foreign-language newspapers.

Many immigrants did become truly American in one sense: the political sense. Acquiring American citizenship was a way to embrace the new country and cut off *allegiance,* or loyalty, to the old. But many of those immigrants did not see any conflict with becoming American citizens and participating in politics and also keeping their old culture. Cultural pluralism developed

despite the efforts of many Americans to convince immigrants that they should adopt Anglo ways.

The Father of Cultural Pluralism

In 1924 philosopher and professor Horace Kallen published *Culture and Democracy in the United States.* In that book Kallen first used a phrase that described his ideal American social philosophy: *cultural pluralism.*

Kallen, a German Jew, had immigrated to Boston with his family in 1887 at the age of five. He later attended Harvard, where he was, in his own words, "a ragged fellow from the other side of the track working his way through." When he first discussed cultural pluralism, Kallen had been developing the concept for more than a decade. In 1915 he had written an essay outlining the ideas that made up the foundation of cultural pluralism. The "Americanization" of immigrants was in full force, and Kallen challenged the desire to make all immigrants fit into the dominant Anglo culture. America's greatest strength, Kallen believed, was what he called "The American Idea," the freedom for people to be different from one another. The idea of cultural pluralism extended that same freedom from individuals to ethnic, religious, and racial groups.

In *Culture and Democracy,* Kallen wrote, "It [the United States] involves a give and take between radically different types, and a mutual respect and mutual cooperation based on mutual understanding." Some Americans welcomed his ideas, especially at a time when *nativist* (anti-immigrant) impulses were strong. One critic, however, said since Kallen was "not American by birth," he lacked the skill "which makes it easy for native Americans to understand one another."

Kallen's ideas, which attacked the cherished symbol of the melting pot, were controversial. They also helped shape a continuing debate on how America's diverse ethnic groups should try to get along.

In the early 20th century some Americans took a more direct approach to assimilation. *Nativists* (those favoring the interests of native-born Americans over the interests of immigrants) wanted to restrict immigration and force existing immigrants to lose their old culture. World War I (1914–1918) brought a greater distrust of immigrants, especially Germans, and "Americanization" became a rallying cry for many native-born Americans. Cultural pluralism as a formal philosophy developed in response to this attempt to force American culture on immigrants and make them deny their own heritage.

The early promoters of cultural pluralism, such as philosopher Horace Kallen, argued that cultural pluralism was already the reality of America's experience with immigrants. More than that, cultural pluralism was something positive, for the members of the different cultural groups represented in the country and for America as a whole. Instead of being a melting pot, Kallen said, the United States was like an orchestra, with each cultural group playing its part to create a symphony of "cultural freedom."

Young members of the Korean Dance Academy prepare for their performance at a Los Angeles festival that celebrates the culture of different Asian groups.

As it developed, cultural pluralism reflected pride in a person's ethnic, racial, or religious background, but it also highlighted immigrant frustration with the Anglo culture's attempt to dominate the country and define who was American. The *Harvard Encyclopedia of American Ethnic Groups* (1980) quotes a Polish-American priest who reflected that feeling: "You English constantly speak as if you were the only Americans, or more American than others.... There is no such thing as an American nation. Poles form a nation, but the United States is a country, under one government, inhabited by representatives of different nations."

For many years the concept of cultural pluralism was mostly the concern of scholars. But in the 1960s, with the rise of the civil rights movement, African Americans began to promote pride in their race. They wanted to study their native African cultures, the unique culture slaves developed in America, and the contributions of those cultures to the larger Anglo culture. A similar impulse developed among Native Americans and other ethnic groups. Cultural pluralism was becoming accepted as the reality in the United States, more so than assimilation—and as a positive reality at that. Behind the push for pluralism was a sense of ethnicity rather than being simply American. More immigrants and descendants of immigrants saw no need to deny their ethnic roots or completely assimilate into the Anglo culture.

■ Ethnicity

Characterization of people based on their ethnic groups (or in some cases racial or religious origins) is called *ethnicity*. For immigrants or their children ethnicity can be a source of pride in their native language, customs, and history. But ethnicity can also be a way for the dominant American society to stereotype immigrants and reinforce the idea that the newcomers are outsiders in the United States. And in recent years some Americans have attacked ethnicity, saying it divides Americans in dangerous ways.

The term *ethnicity* was first used in the 20th century, usually by critics of the notion that the United States was a melting pot. The people argued that immigrants, even after they become American citizens, retain their ethnic identity and *should* retain it. Keeping some loyalty to their old ways of life does not contradict being a good American.

Although the term might be fairly new, the idea of ethnicity is as old as immigration to America. By living in towns or neighborhoods with others from their homelands, immigrants kept alive their sense of ethnic identity. Foreign-language newspapers, social support groups, celebrations of national festivals—all helped keep ethnicity strong in the United States. For some groups, such as the Irish Catholics and the Jews, religious beliefs and ceremonies were also closely intertwined with the sense of ethnicity.

Many immigrants never had to consider their ethnicity before coming to America. At home, for the most part, they were surrounded by people who spoke the same language, had the same values, and most likely practiced the same religion. But in America an immigrant was thrown together with people from many lands, as well as with native-born Americans. The Anglo Americans tended to lump together all the newcomers from one country or region, which helped spark a sense of ethnic identity. That identity also gave immigrants a sense of strength and a support system as they adjusted to life in their new homes.

As years pass, immigrants and their children may lose some sense of their ethnicity or create a new ethnic identity shaped by their experiences in America. In their book *Beyond the Melting Pot* (1963) Nathan Glazer and Daniel Patrick Moynihan suggested that Italian Americans (or other ethnic groups) had little in common with friends or relatives back home. "In America they were a distinctive group that maintained itself, was identifiable, and gave something to those who identified with it."

The Elite "Ethnic" Group

Settlers from England were the dominant European ethnic group in America during colonial times, and their culture was the biggest influence on what became American culture. The elite class of America shared many traits: their white race, roots in Great Britain, and a Protestant religion. Those traits led to the name *WASP* (white Anglo-Saxon Protestant) to describe the group. (*Anglo-Saxon* refers to the Angles and Saxons, tribes from Germany that invaded England in the 5th and 6th centuries.)

By the 1980s social scientists noted that ethnicity seemed on the decline among most descendants of European immigrants. (This decline is less true for the recent immigrants arriving in large numbers from Asia and Latin America.) New arrivals from Europe or small groups devoted to the old ways might try to keep the original ethnic identity strong, but the more assimilated European ethnics are not regularly in touch with the cultures of their homelands. But even for the most assimilated immigrants, there is usually some tie to their heritage. Italians, for example, might add a pasta dish to their, Thanksgiving dinners. To some Hispanic Americans, January 6—Three Kings Day—is as important as Christmas and is celebrated in the United States with gift giving and a special meal.

WASP (see "The Elite 'Ethnic' Group" sidebar) is often used in an insulting way by ethnic or racial groups that feel they are discriminated against by the dominant Anglo society. WASPs are sometimes stereotyped as unemotional, wealthy, and snobbish. Not all people who are white, Protestant, and have Anglo-Saxon roots fit this stereotype, and not all members of the political and economic elite in the United States are WASPs. But for much of American history WASPs were the leaders of the country—and the people who discriminated against the other ethnic groups that followed them to America.

These Russian-American children from Brooklyn, New York, wear costumes from their homeland during a 1997 celebration of Russian culture.

▇ Ethnicity as a Negative

Ethnicity can give immigrants a sense of identity and history as they undergo the difficult process of adjusting to life in the United States. It can also, however, mark them as outsiders. Since colonial days Americans have often classified immigrants by their ethnic origins or religious beliefs and discriminated against them on that basis. One scholar suggests that this negative ethnicity "has its origins in conquest, slavery, and exploitation of foreign labor." Racial and ethnic inequality were the result.

In 1698 South Carolina offered a cash payment to immigrants who settled in that colony. But one ethnic group— the Scotch-Irish—and one religious group—the Roman Catholics—were not included in this program. In the 1840s the phrase *No Irish need apply* was common on signs advertising job opportunities. (African Americans later faced the same kind of discrimination.) To the dominant social groups, certain ethnic groups were unwanted or had undesirable characteristics. But Americans made some exceptions within large immigrant groups. In 1911 a congressional report made a distinction between northern and southern Italians. The "good" northern Italians were hardworking and law-abiding, and the "bad" southern Italians (especially Sicilians) were lazy and tended to become involved in crime. Currently, the stereotype of Sicilians (and Italians in general) as members of crime organizations often remains.

Because of those kinds of prejudice, some immigrants have felt compelled to deny their racial or ethnic origins. In the past light-skinned African Americans sometimes tried to pass as whites, and many immigrants have changed their names to sound less foreign and more American. The recent push to honor ethnic identity is partially a response to the pressure some immigrants have felt to deny their heritage.

▇ Multiculturalism

As cultural pluralism and ethnicity received more favorable attention beginning in the 1960s, their supporters felt the U.S. education system needed to reflect the country's racial and ethnic diversity and put more emphasis on the contribution of minorities in the United States. This new thrust in education is called *multiculturalism*. The goal of multiculturalism is to show the past accomplishments of all races and ethnic groups in the United States and promote tolerance among its citizens today.

Multiculturalism began as a direct response to the melting pot ideas of the past. In 1972 an association of colleges that train many of the country's teachers offered this view:

> Multicultural education rejects the view that schools should seek to melt away cultural differences or the view that schools should merely tolerate cultural pluralism…. Multicultural education recognizes cultural diversity as a fact of life in American society and it affirms that this cultural diversity is a valuable exercise that should be preserved and extended.

In 1974 the supporters of ethnicity and multiculturalism persuaded Congress to pass the Ethnic Heritage Studies Program Act. This law called for greater research on ethnic groups and their contributions to the United States and pushed for teaching about those accomplishments in schools.

Bilingualism

Along with multiculturalism, some educators pushed for *bilingual education*—using an immigrant's native language in the classroom along with English. Congress passed the country's first law promoting bilingual education in 1967. Until then most immigrants encountered a "sink-or-swim" approach in U.S. schools: classes were taught exclusively in English, and students had to struggle along until they developed their English skills. Bilingualism was primarily targeted at Spanish-speaking students, but communities with large immigrant populations who spoke other languages also had bilingual programs. Such programs continue today.

■ Reaction to Cultural Pluralism

Some scholars fear the rise of multiculturalism and the emphasis on ethnicity. Many studies of bilingual education show it might not be an effective way to make immigrants fluent in English or to teach other subjects.

Others see multiculturalism as an attack on American values. Bob Dole, a former U.S. senator and presidential candidate, said in 1995, "We must stop the practice of multilingual education as a means of instilling ethnic pride or as a therapy for low self-esteem or out of elitist guilt over a culture built on the traditions of the West."

Three Kings Day, January 6, marks the end of the Christmas holiday in many Hispanic countries, and the day is often celebrated by Hispanic Americans as well. This Three Kings Day parade was held in New York.

Although some scholars see the attacks on bilingual education and multiculturalism as part of a "new nativism," even some minorities argue that such programs do not help immigrants succeed in American society. In a 1997 *Los Angeles Times* poll 83 percent of Hispanic parents opposed bilingual education.

Questioning the role of ethnicity in the United States is not new. President Theodore Roosevelt saw a danger in "hyphenated Americans"—people who identified themselves as Polish-American people, Japanese-American people, and so on—instead of as simply Americans. At the end of the 20th century the defense of ethnicity and cultural pluralism has led some people to warn of deeper separations between the different cultural and racial groups in the United States. When cultural pluralism is carried too far, the critics say, the separation of cultural groups threatens the sense of unity that has been so important throughout the history of the country.

Some supporters of ethnicity and cultural pluralism, however, say that sense of unity has always been more of a myth than a reality. Others argue for a middle ground, saying Americans can keep their sense of ethnicity and still be part of a whole, still be American. According to historian Arthur Schlesinger Jr., "The genius of America lies in its capacity to forge a single nation from peoples of remarkably diverse racial, religious, and ethnic origins." The challenge to balance the diversity and the unity in a just way is a constant theme in American history.

Ellis Island Museum Oral History Project

NAME: George Zemanovic
COUNTRY: Czechoslovakia
YEAR IMMIGRATED: 1922
AGE: 6 years
INTERVIEWER: Paul E. Sigrist Jr.

SIGRIST: Tell me about what you did the first night in America.

ZEMANOVIC: Slept without this thumping sound that we were… exposed to for ten days and nights and whatever. And then there … were some young children, my peers, you know, and they, we tried to communicate. What, what, of course I knew only Slovak, and these kids I think may have known some Slovak also because they were Slovak family there. And they introduced me to chewing gum, which was to me the most horrible tasting thing that I had ever experienced…. I tried desperately to try and be a part of the group by chewing gum, and I just couldn't tolerate it. It would nauseate me. So I found a happy way to get around it. I would just take a slice of raw bacon and chew on that, and chew on it and chew on it and chew on it, and then I felt part of the group. You have to understand that … fat was very scarce … in these farming communities. Fat was … any fat was very, very choice. I mean you safeguarded it. You didn't throw anything away. I remember my sister and I arguing and fighting over the marrow from soup bones. How delicious it was. I remember my mother making toast and spreading lard over it. And that to us was a treat, that we were so starved for fats over there … and then something that I didn't really learn until my mother told us.…"You know," she says, "Oh, we had very little meat." Even though … you live on a farm, meats were only served during festive occasions and holidays. Everything was just plain fare, and you used a little fat to provide a little sauce and whatever, and [pauses] whatever you called it, I don't remember the American term— *sacmaska,* they called it. You always took a little fat, and you took flour, and … you browned it, and you made sort of a gravy. I guess that's the term, *gravy.* And that was … about all of the fat that people had to eat, and so…

SIGRIST: So this was the first thing that struck you.…

ZEMANOVIC: Yeah. Yeah.…

SIGRIST: America being different than Czechoslovakia. Suddenly you have…

ZEMANOVIC: And then ice cream also. I mean I loved ice cream. That was delicious. And, of course, as I said, we had a few samples of it on the boat and Ellis Island, but [pauses] the Americanized food was a novelty to us, you know, and…

SIGRIST: Had your father learned English?

ZEMANOVIC: He knew a few phrases. But in that one year that he was here he was able to … communicate with, with basic words. And actually it … became my responsibility, and I learned English very quickly, to act as an interpreter. Actually I recall that … after I learned the basic English words that I did most of the translating or explaining or whatever had to be done.…

I was also confused because I was six years, and they put me into kindergarten. Of course, you know, I had no knowledge of [the] English language, so I remember assembling little pieces of paper into … you know, basket weaving and stuff like that. And in a few months, why, then they moved me to another class where we started to read. And I was trying to learn the English language, and the teachers were being very patient. And one of things that I was very confused about was they were reading about Little Red Riding Hood and Peter Rabbit and all these other things, and these animals were talking, you know. And I came home, I said, "Mom," I said, "I don't understand.… We had animals all the time, and I never heard any talk. And here I'm reading about these animals talking." And she said, "Don't worry.… You'll understand everything. Just learn." And so [he laughs] that was one of the things that I can recall. And I can still recall my first Christmas tree. Oh, what an elaborate thing it was. This was an assembly for Christmas. And all the children got down and sang Christmas carols, and it was just beautiful. Of course, we had trees in Czechoslovakia in Dolna Suca. They were little, little conifers with a couple of candles stuck on them and stuff. They celebrated Christmas there very, very simply. And so this was my first real American lit-up Christmas tree, with all the tinsel and all the electric lights and everything you could imagine. So that was quite a, that left quite an impression on me.

SIGRIST: Do you remember your first English word, or when the lightbulb sort of went off, and it all started making sense?

ZEMANOVIC: [pauses] Well, I can't, I can't really say there was any one.... I had difficulty in school between the singular and the plural. I remember one of the things that I was always being corrected when we spoke, "Peter Rabbits." And ... they said, "No, no Peter Rabbit. One." And I would say "rabbits" because of course at the time I knew nothing about plural, and, you know, and singular, and whatever else, but ... I'm trying to think. I'm sure there had to be something that, that hit me, but—chewing gum was probably the first thing that came my way [he laughs], because everybody talked chewing gum. Everybody was chaw— you know, chewing gum, you know. What—what else can I say? [He laughs.]

SIGRIST: Tell me about your mother getting adjusted to this country. And tell me a little bit maybe about her first year here, and what that was like for her.

ZEMANOVIC: It, our first year was miserable. My father found a cold water flat not too far away from the place where he was rooming. And so that at least we had some people we knew that we could visit and ask questions and whatever else. And we were about three or four blocks away from where these people that my father was living— where my father was living, and so. But this was a cold water flat and it had a woodstove in the kitchen. And I can still remember my mother and father in the snow cutting wood with a cross-cut saw in the yard. And all the neighbors I understand were horrified at how my father was working my mother, you know, to, to, I don't know where he got the wood from, or anything. Obviously

they were big logs. And he must have borrowed the saw so we could cut, cut. I don't know if we had coal, if we bought coal. It was simply ... you know, one of these 50-pound bags or buckets or something. And it was cold. And it was, it was, only gas—gas illumination, gas— gas cooking....

SIGRIST: What do you remember about having gaslight in the house? What sticks out in your mind about that?

ZEMANOVIC: I had one horrible experience with gaslight in this particular apartment, flat if you want to call it.... One of the boys that was my peer, who I befriended or who befriended us,...he was [pauses] very careless. And what he did was, he got some paper, and I was trying to light, I was trying to light the gaslight in the bathroom. And he got a wad of paper, and he lit it and it caught fire. And he dropped it, and I think it started fire in the bathroom, and I was desperate. I can still remember how I desperately tried to beat this fire out and stomp on it so that it wouldn't set the place on fire. And ... I think, I succeeded in putting the fire out, but it made me very, very angry with this carelessness of ... this chap, this other kid who just thought it was a lark. 'Cause I was desperately afraid that my father would find out about it, and, and, you know, there would be all sorts of horrible recriminations and whatever. He would put up with no nonsense. But I must say that our first winter here in this country was really miserable. And to make matters worse I had, I had gone through an episode of measles.... Right after I started school I caught measles and I had to miss school for about a month [pauses] getting over the case of measles.

... I don't know if we were vaccinated. I suppose we were, but not against, I don't know, whatever it was....

SIGRIST: So for your poor mother on top of having to cope with all this new world she's got an ill child....

ZEMANOVIC: She's got an ill child, and [pauses] not knowing the language, and ... in a strange land, no neighbors who could, you know. The particular place where there was a very grumpy lady living who would not associate with us. It was a [pauses] inhospitable neighborhood is all I can remember. I can remember running around in— they were doing some house building in the neighborhood—picking up scrap pieces of wood, bringing them home for kindling for the fire and whatever else....

SIGRIST: In their own way they're still sort of living a rural existence, I think...

ZEMANOVIC: Yeah, we were self-sufficient so to speak. You know we tried to be self-sufficient. There was, at that time there was ... no aid and assistance, public assistance or anything like that. And even if it was offered, I don't think my father would take it. He was always very, very independent. He wasn't going to be a beggar, you know. And anybody who accepted assistance like that [pauses] he would lower his self-esteem. He was poor, but he still had pride.

SEE ALSO: Assimilation; Education; Ethnicity; Language Issues; Literature, the Media, and Ethnicity; Prejudice and Discrimination

CULTURE

Culture is the behaviors, beliefs, and products of a group of people at a given time. Many things are part of a society's culture, including arts, skills, customs, language, religion, and political systems, as well as such material goods as tools, food, and clothing. Culture entails learned behaviors passed down from one generation to the next.

The term *culture* can apply to a small group of people, such as a family or a neighborhood; it can also apply to very large groups of people, such as nations or ethnic groups. One can even talk about a global culture or the culture of humanity.

Two young Jewish children take pride in their culture during a parade in New York City.

■ American Culture

American culture, like other cultures, is constantly changing. Two centuries ago America's dominating culture reflected a white, Protestant, male-dominated society. In the early 1800s each group of immigrants that arrived in the United States brought along a culture very different from the one that existed in the new country.

As immigrant and American cultures came into contact with one another, both changed. The immigrants slowly *assimilated* into, or adapted to, life in the United States; they took on the language as well as many of the customs and practices of the new country. However, American culture was also altered by the immigrants.

Culture includes music, dance, and other art forms. Girls help keep a centuries-old dance tradition alive during a St. Patrick's Day parade in New York City.

The new arrivals brought new types of food, such as hot dogs, hamburgers, pizza, and tacos. They added new genres of music, creating gospel, blues, and jazz. They altered American attitudes, introducing a more easygoing manner to the formerly Puritan way of thinking. Immigrants also affected politics, religion, education, and even the "American" language. Examples of foreign words that have found their way into everyday usage in the United States include the French words *déjà vu* (DAY-zhah VOO), *hors d'oeuvre* (OR DERV), and *beret* (beh-RAY) and the Spanish words *adobe* (ah-DOH-bee), *tornado,* and *rodeo.* Other words from foreign

languages include *kindergarten* (from German), *futon* (from Japanese), and *pajamas* (from Hindi, a language spoken in India).

■ Cultural Pluralism

The combining of cultures in the United States was first described in 1782 as a sort of "melting pot" by French author Michel-Guillaume-Jean de Crèvecoeur (who wrote under the American name J. Hector St. John). In *Letters from an American Farmer,* he wrote,

What then is the American, this new man? He is either a European, or the descendant of a European, hence the strange mixture of blood, which you will find in no other country. He is an American, who, leaving behind him all his ancient prejudices and manners, receives new ones from the new mode of life he has embraced…. Here individuals of all races are melted into a new race of men, whose labours and posterity will one day cause great changes in the world.

In 1908 British author Israel Zangwill first used the phrase *melting pot* to describe American culture in a play titled *The Melting-Pot.*

In recent years the melting pot image has fallen out of favor. Many people prefer to highlight our nation's rich and diverse cultural heritage, teaching tolerance and respect for other cultures while encouraging immigrants to adopt some attitudes and customs of the Anglo culture. This philosophy, known as *cultural pluralism* or *cultural democracy,* has led some people to drop the term *melting pot* in favor of a different description: American culture as a stew, with many different ingredients all retaining their unique identities while adding flavor to the whole.

American culture continues to evolve. Immigrants from Asia, Latin America, and other places have an effect today. Telecommunications and the computer superhighway are also changing U.S. culture as people come in contact with others all around the world.

SEE ALSO: Assimilation; Cultural Pluralism; Ethnicity; Race

CZECHS

Czechs are Slavic people who live in the Czech Republic, located in the heart of central Europe. The Czech Republic is made up of the regions known as Bohemia in the east, Moravia in the west, and Czech Silesia in the north. During the earliest days of Czech immigration to the United States, Czech immigrants were often called Bohemians, Moravians, or Silesians, depending on which region they came from.

Although some Czechs lived in America as early as the 1630s, the bulk of Czech immigrants entered the United States during the great influx of immigrants in the late 1800s and early 1900s. Czech immigrants came to be known as hardworking, independent people, committed to life in the new land but also actively interested in happenings in their homeland. Czechs brought with them a love of music, art, and learning.

■ History

The area known as the Czech Republic was first settled by Slavs in the 5th and 6th centuries. In the 9th century the Moravians had a powerful kingdom, the Great Moravian Empire, which included Poland, Bohemia, and part of Hungary. However, in 906 the empire was destroyed, and the strength and importance of Bohemia began to increase.

In the mid-1300s Holy Roman Emperor Charles IV made the Bohemian city of Prague, the present-day capital of the Czech Republic, his seat of residence. While Charles IV was in power, Prague was a center of European culture. In 1526, however, Bohemia and Moravia came under the control of the Austrian Habsburg monarchy. The Czechs revolted in 1620 but were defeated by the Austrians. For the next three centuries the two regions were ruled by Austria's monarchs.

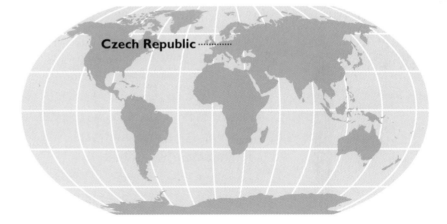

At the end of World War I (1914–1918) the Austro-Hungarian Empire was dissolved. The Czechs and their neighbors to the south, the Slovaks, united to form the independent state of Czechoslovakia. During World War II (1939–1945) Czechoslovakia lost its independence to Nazi Germany. After the war a Communist-dominated government took power in Czechoslovakia.

In 1948 the Communists gained total control of Czechoslovakia. Many intellectuals and professionals fled Czechoslovakia after the Communist takeover. In the late 1960s many Czech officials tried to reform the Communist government. In response, Soviet troops invaded Czechoslovakia and reinforced the Soviet style of government. Another wave of refugees fled the nation.

In 1989 the people of Czechoslovakia began to rebel against the Communist government. In December of that year a new, multiparty government was established, and playwright Václav Havel became president. Although there were ethnic conflicts between the Czechs and the Slovaks, Czechoslovakia remained united as one nation until January 1, 1993. On that date Czechoslovakia peacefully split into two separate nations: the Czech Republic (Bohemia, Moravia, and Czech Silesia) and Slovakia.

▣ Coming to America

The first Czech immigrants arrived in America as early as the 1630s. Many of those immigrants were Protestant Czechs escaping religious persecution in their homeland, which was ruled by the Catholic Habsburg monarchs. Many fled first to Sweden and Holland, traveling from those countries to the New World.

Despite the Czechs' early arrival, probably no more than 500 Czech

The First Czech Immigrant

The first Czech immigrant recorded in America was Augustine Herrman, who arrived in New Amsterdam in 1633. Herrman, a skilled cartographer, was the first person to map the growing city that would later become New York City. He also prepared maps of Virginia and Maryland, which were used for the next two centuries. In 1660 Herrman was given 20,000 acres of land in Maryland by Lord Baltimore for his map services.

immigrants came to the United States over the next 200 years. The year 1850, however, marked the beginning of a large wave of Czech immigration. Between 1850 and 1914 more than 350,000 Czechs arrived in the United States.

A number of factors served to push or pull the huge flood of Czech immigrants to the United States. Some Czechs were attracted by stories of economic opportunity: land, gold, freedom, and democracy. Others left to avoid serving in the Austrian army. Getting out of the homeland and to the United States also became easier. In the homeland barriers to immigration, such as restrictions on people who wanted to leave the country and high passport taxes, were removed. And the invention of the steamship reduced a perilous, months-long voyage to a somewhat less dangerous trip that took two to three weeks. As pressures at home mounted—economic depression, crop failures, war—more and more Czechs looked to the United States for a fresh start.

During the great wave of Czech immigration to the United States in the late 1800s, most immigrants arrived with their families and little else. The usual baggage of a Czech immigrant included clothes, a feather mattress, and a little money. Czech immigrants, however, generally arrived with more money than did other immigrants. In 1902, for example, the average declaration per Czech immigrant was $23.12, compared with $14.84 for immigrants from other countries. The extra money made it easier for Czechs to leave the busy ports of entry and continue on to the Midwest. It wasn't long before Czech immigrants began carving a place for themselves in U.S. history.

In the mid-20th century smaller waves of Czech immigrants arrived in the United States. Those groups were different from the first great wave of Czech immigrants. Instead of seeking economic opportunity, many of the immigrants were fleeing religious and political persecution. In the 1930s, for example, a small number of Jews left Czechoslovakia before the Nazis took over. In 1948 and again in 1968 thousands of immigrants, mostly intellectuals and professionals, fled Czechoslovakia during Communist crackdowns.

■ Life in America

The Czech immigrants who arrived in the United States in the late 1800s and early 1900s came to stay. The large majority of Czech immigrants during this time were part of family groups, especially in the early years. More than two-thirds were women and children. Few of the immigrants ever returned to their homeland. Between 1908 and 1910 the return rate for Czechs was just 11 percent.

Czech immigrants included people from nearly every walk of life: musicians, doctors, artisans, brewers, professors, journalists, scientists, farmers, soldiers, and revolutionaries all made their way across the Atlantic to the United States.

Like other immigrants, many of the new Czech arrivals—nearly half—settled in big cities. In the late 1800s Chicago, New York City, and Cleveland all had large Czech populations. Other Czech immigrants headed west to places such as Wisconsin, Texas, Nebraska, Iowa, and Minnesota, where they purchased land for farming.

The Czech immigrants had the education and skills to adapt easily to their new homeland. They quickly became known for their hard work, honesty, and love of music. Czech immigrants did not, however, *assimilate* (adopt American ways) quickly. Some had difficulty learning the English language, a language much different from their own. In fact, many Czech immigrants chose to settle near Germans, their traditional enemies, because they spoke similar languages.

Some Americans accused the Czechs of being "clannish," of sticking with others of their culture instead of trying to integrate into the American culture. This was, to an extent, true. As more and more Czech immigrants journeyed to the United States, they settled in ethnic neighborhoods and opened shops, taverns, and churches. They also quickly formed organizations and societies. The Czech neighborhoods and organizations enabled the immigrants to hold on to their language and culture longer than other groups.

At an ethnic festival in Masaryktown, Florida, a group of Czechs dance the beseda. Beseda is a form of Czech square dancing that became popular around 1900 "as a means of unifying what later became Czechoslovakia through dance." It consists of many small dances from several regions.

Despite their desire to set up ethnic organizations and maintain the culture of their homeland, Czech immigrants were quick to immerse their children into the culture of the United States—the public schools. The Czechs brought with them a long tradition of respect for learning and education, and the attendance of Czech immigrant children in English-speaking public schools was high. Although some Czech-language *parochial* (parish-run) schools were set up in New York City, Chicago, Cleveland, and St. Louis, most Czech immigrants sent their children to public schools. To ensure that the language, culture, and history of the Old World was not completely lost, some immigrants sent their children to supplemental Czech-language schools after public school hours and on weekends.

Cyrus Cacioppo of Swisher, Iowa, stands beside plum trees planted by Joseph Stodola, an immigrant from Bohemia in the 1880s. Stodola hid a small plum tree in his clothing when he came to the United States.

Urban Life

Czech immigrants had settled in New York City since the arrival of Augustine Herrman in 1633. (See "The First Czech Immigrant" sidebar on page 42.)

Although New York City retained a large Czech population through the 1800s and 1900s, later arrivals settled in other cities as well, most notably Chicago. The first Czech immigrants arrived there in 1846. By 1900 the city was the second largest Czech urban center in the world after Prague, with 50,000 Czechs living there.

The Czechs, like other immigrant groups, found that life in the big cities of the United States was not easy. One Czech immigrant arrived penniless in Chicago with his wife and eight children. He built his first home out of abandoned railroad ties, using dirt to cover the roof. The hut had no windows and no chimney to vent the old oven that served as a heater. Not surprisingly the home burned down, leaving the family homeless for a time.

Czech immigrants, known as "the Yankees of Europe" for their strong work ethic, engaged in all kinds of trades. They took manufacturing, mechanical, and trade jobs. They were especially prevalent as tailors in Chicago's garment industry. The city's *Directory of Bohemian Merchants, Traders, and Societies* (1900) listed hundreds of Czech store owners and tradesmen in the city.

As time passed, many Czech immigrants in Chicago became doctors, teachers, lawyers, journalists, and musicians. By the 1920s Czechs also were prominent in the banking industry, controlling 15 state and federal banks. Many purchased homes in the city and its surrounding areas.

In New York City Czech immigrants settled first on the Lower East Side, along with thousands of immigrants from other countries. Most Czechs in New York City took jobs as cigar makers. In 1865 as many as 95 percent of Czech workers labored in factories or at home, making cigars. (See "The Bohemian Cigar Makers" sidebar on page 46.) Those who worked at cigar making earned anywhere from $3 to $12 a week, wages similar to those earned in other immigrant-dominated occupations. Cigar making was a common job for Czech women through the 1900s; two-thirds of Czech women and half their working daughters made cigars.

In December 1904 *Charities,* a social welfare journal of the time, ran a report titled "The Bohemian Women in New York." It described the immigrants from Czechoslovakia:

> The Bohemians are perhaps the cleanest of the poor people in the city, and they struggle manfully against the bad conditions of the New York tenement houses. They are fortunate in being intensely musical, and they find great joy in the occasional dance or picnic. They are a hard-working people, and both the women and children are often overworked. The girls marry with the expectation of continuing their hard life in the factory.

By the 1920s most Czechs were no longer involved in the cigar making industry.

Another trade that was prominent among Czech immigrants in New York City was the production of pearl buttons. In the 1920s about half of all pearl buttons made in the United States were made in Czech shops.

Czech Farmers

The first important rural Czech settlements were founded in Wisconsin in 1848. The climate and terrain in that state were similar to those in the Czech homeland, and Wisconsin became a top destination for Czech immigrants. By 1860 one-third of all Czech immigrants were living in Wisconsin. A decade later the state had the largest population of Czechs in the nation.

Czech immigrants arrived in the Midwest at a time when the United States was encouraging the settlement and farming of land there. In 1862 the Homestead Act allowed citizens and immigrants who intended to become citizens to acquire 160 acres of public land for a small filing fee. Homesteaders had to be willing to live on the land for five years. By 1900 about 600,000 settlers—including many Czechs—had received title to about 80 million acres.

Life for the would-be farmer was every bit as difficult as life for the newly arrived city dweller. The following description of Czech settlers is from "Bohemian Farmers in Wisconsin," published in a December 1904 issue of *Charities:*

> The early settler bought from forty to sixty acres of land, making

U.S. Secretary of State Madeleine Albright visits towns in Bohemia in 1997. Albright's ancestors immigrated to the United States from Czechoslovakia.

only a small cash payment, and giving a mortgage for the rest.... With the help of his neighbors, who blazed trails as they came lest they should not be able to find the way back, he built a log cabin and felled a few trees to give space for a vegetable patch. Then came the serious work of clearing the land, and at the same time earning enough outside money to live and pay part of the debt.

Despite the hardship, Czech immigrants succeeded at agriculture. They grew a variety of crops, including rye, wheat, corn, oats, and potatoes. They also produced maple syrup. In 1877 a Wisconsin historian recorded his

thoughts about Czech immigrants: "They were distinguished by their jovial temperament and fondness of music and song. As farmers they were diligent, steady, and ready to put new ideas into practice."

From Wisconsin Czech immigrants spread westward to Nebraska, Minnesota, Iowa, and Kansas. Others moved straight from their homeland to the rich agricultural areas of Texas. By 1900 a third of all Czechs in the United States were in agriculture. By 1970, however, that had changed. Few Czechs were employed in farming; instead, many held white-collar jobs.

Czech Societies and Organizations

The first Czech-American society in the United States was the Czecho-Slavic Society, founded in 1850 in New York City by a group of freethinkers. Freethinkers believed in science and rational thought over faith and religious beliefs. Some freethinkers were especially critical of the Catholic religion, which had been imposed on the Czech people by the Austrian Habsburg monarchy. The new group, whose headquarters were in a tavern, assisted new arrivals from the homeland. The group lasted just two years.

One of the most important Czech societies was the Czech-Slavonic Benevolent Society, whose acronym in Czech is CSPS. The CSPS, founded in St. Louis, Missouri, in 1854, charged 50 cents a month for health insurance and funeral benefits. The group also supported orphans and elderly people; built national halls for concerts, plays, and other social functions; and sponsored cultural and educational

"The Bohemian Cigar Makers"

In 1890 Jacob Riis, an immigrant to the United States from Denmark, wrote the following in a book titled *How the Other Half Lives*:

Men, women and children work together seven days in the week in these cheerless tenements to make a living for the family, from the break of day till far into the night. Often the wife is the original cigarmaker from the old home, the husband having adopted her trade here as a matter of necessity, because, knowing no word of English, he could get [no] other work....

Riis also described working conditions of Bohemian cigar makers on the Lower East Side of New York City in his book:

Take a row of houses in East Tenth Street as an instance. They contained thirty-five families of cigarmakers, with probably not half a dozen persons in the whole lot of them, outside of the children, who could speak a word of English, though many had been [in] the country half a lifetime. This room with two windows giving on the street, and a rear attachment without windows, called a bedroom by courtesy, is rented at $12.25 a month. In the front room man and wife work at the bench from six in the morning till nine at night. They make a team, stripping the tobacco leaves together; then he makes the filler, and she rolls the wrapper on and finishes the cigar. For a thousand they receive $3.75, and can turn out together three thousand cigars a week.

events. Like the fraternal organizations of many other immigrant groups, the CSPS also strongly encouraged its members to adapt to the American culture. In 1933 CSPS became the Czechoslovak Society of America (CSA). The CSA is the oldest continuous fraternal benefit society in the United States.

Women, who couldn't join the CSPS unless they were wives of members, were forced to turn elsewhere. So many started their own groups. A handful of important Czech women's organizations existed in the 1800s and early 1900s. The largest was the Union of Czech Women, formed in Cleveland, Ohio, in 1870. By 1920 the group had 23,000 members.

Many ethnic organizations were patterned on similar groups in the homeland. Examples are groups known as the Slavic Linden societies that sprang up in 1857 and later. The Slavic Linden societies founded libraries and night schools, organized theater groups and choral groups, and sponsored lectures and other cultural and social functions.

Other groups patterned after those in the homeland were the gymnastic societies known as Sokols (Falcons). The first Sokol chapter was started in Prague in 1862. Three years later the first American branch was founded in St. Louis. Sokols promoted Czech culture and patriotism education through physical, moral, and intellectual development. Sokol *slets,* gatherings at which members exercise to music and take part in sports and other activities, were first held in 1879 and have been held every four years since.

Music and the arts, integral parts of Czech culture in the homeland, played an important part in the life of Czech

immigrants in the United States. One observer of Czech immigrants noted that almost every Czech home had a musical instrument. A common Slavic saying that found its way to the United States was "Every Czech a musician." The Czechs in America organized bands, orchestras, and choirs and in 1885 built the Bohemian Opera House in Manitowok, Wisconsin. In Chicago the Czechs opened a professional theater company, Ludvik's Theatrical Troupe, which performed until the 1930s.

Czech Immigration to the United States

By 1850 about 10,000 Czechs lived in the United States. The peak of Czech immigration, however, was yet to come.

Decade	Number of Immigrants
1850–1860	23,009
1861–1870	33,123
1871–1880	52,079
1881–1890	62,050
1891–1900	42,711
1901–1910	94,516
1911–1920	41,995
1921–1930	27,296
1931–1940	1,682
1941–1950	14,969
1951–1960	28,808
1961–1970	21,448

SOURCES: *Harvard Encyclopedia of Ethnic Groups* (1980); *The Czechs in America, 1633–1977* (1978)

In the 1900s Czech immigration to the United States was at an all-time high, and the new arrivals kept the rolls of the fraternal societies and other organizations full. By 1920 there were approximately 2,500 Czech-American organizations, 500 in Chicago alone. The organizations included fraternal and benevolent societies, religious groups, Sokol chapters, labor and union organizations, and cultural clubs.

However, the 1920s also marked the beginning of a decline of ethnicity in the Czech community. The immigration quota imposed in 1924 reduced the number of Czechs allowed to immigrate to the United States to 3,073 per year;

A mother and daughter wear traditional Czech costumes at the opening of the Czech and Slovak Museum in Cedar Rapids, Iowa, in October 1995. The opening was attended by President Bill Clinton as well as by the presidents of the Czech Republic and Slovakia.

in 1929 that number was further reduced to 2,874. The Great Depression of the 1930s forced many Czech organizations and institutions in the United States out of business. As people lost their jobs and homes, the organizations lost dues-paying members. After the 1930s fewer ethnic Czech organizations existed. In addition, second-generation Czechs were not as interested as their parents and grandparents had been in keeping the culture of the homeland alive.

Although Czech immigrants were concerned about maintaining their culture and ethnicity, they considered themselves 100 percent American. A 1910 survey of urban Czech family heads who had been in the United

States ten years or more found that 80 percent had been *naturalized*—made legal citizens—and 13 percent had their first papers. By 1910 two-thirds of first-generation Czech immigrants spoke English—another sign that Czechs were assimilating.

Czech immigrants remained loyal and connected to their homeland. The first of a number of organized trips back to the homeland was held in 1885. Czechoslovakia encouraged the visits and worked to promote tourism to Czechs living abroad. And Czech musicians, authors, politicians, and journalists often traveled from the homeland to lecture in the United States. One such visitor was famed composer Antonin Dvorak, who composed his final symphony, "From the New World," while in the United States.

Czech Americans during the World Wars

World War I gave Czech immigrants the opportunity to support the homeland in word and deed. At the beginning of the war Czech immigrants held rallies against Austrian aggression in Serbia. Because of their outspoken condemnation of German aggression, Czech Americans did not suffer as much as some other groups (notably German Americans) from the anti-immigrant hysteria that was sweeping the nation during the war.

Czech immigrants raised hundreds of thousands of dollars in funds and relief during the war. The Czech National Alliance, founded in 1914 in Chicago, played an important part in collecting funds and organizing support. Czech Americans were also vocal in their desire for an independent Czech state. They lobbied tirelessly to sway popular opinion in the United States toward this end.

Czech-American citizens even acted as spies during World War I, ferrying messages between Czech patriots and British intelligence agents. One such Czech-American patriot was Emanuel Voska. Voska delivered messages from Prague to British intelligence agents in London. In the United States he organized a network of Czech immigrants who worked in Austrian and German embassies, businesses, and private homes. The Czechs intercepted mail and reported anything that might be of use to the United States and its Allies. Voska's network was a valuable source of information for the Allies.

During World War II Czech Americans again proved vital to the war effort. Working to help Czechoslovakia, which was under Nazi control, they raised hundreds of thousands of dollars in relief funds for the homeland. Each month the Czech National Council, a Czech-American organization, published *News Flashes from Czechoslovakia* to inform Czech Americans on the situation in the homeland. The bulletin had a peak circulation of 25,000. The council also supplied aid to refugees and soldiers fighting for Allied troops.

Czechs in America Today

The 1990 Census reported that 1,296,000 people of Czech ancestry were living in the United States. More than half (52 percent) lived in the Midwest. Despite the decline of Czech ethnicity in the United States, a number of Czech organizations and societies are still active, especially in areas with large Czech populations. Recently, for example, the Czech Museum and Archive opened in Cedar Rapids, Iowa. Czech festivals are held in the Midwest and in Texas. A number of Czech cultural sites exist on the Internet.

Famous Czech Americans include Secretary of State Madeleine Albright, Apollo astronaut Eugene Cernan, director Milos Forman, professional basketball player John Havlicek, tennis player Martina Navritalova, and the first American male saint, John Nepomucene Neumann.

 Ellis Island Museum Oral History Project

NAME: George Zemanovic
COUNTRY: Czechoslovakia
YEAR IMMIGRATED: 1922
AGE: 6 years
INTERVIEWER: Paul E. Sigrist Jr.

SIGRIST: Now, when you were in Czechoslovakia, did you have any perception of what America was?

Performers from the Czech Republic dance in the streets of Silver Dollar City, Missouri, during the World-Fest in 1998. The World-Fest is the largest international festival in the United States.

ZEMANOVIC: None, whatsoever. I didn't even know there was … America. … I don't know how old I was, but apparently I must have been at least four and a half or five … when I first saw … my first vehicle that didn't have a horse or ox connected to it. I saw this so-called wagon moving down the highway with soldiers standing in it, and there was nothing pulling it, and yet it was moving. And I was horror-stricken. I ran home in horror telling my mother what I just saw.… I knew very little of why my father would be leaving. At the time it was beyond my ken, let's say, you know. I was a five-year-old kid.…

SIGRIST: Well, let's get you to America. Do you remember packing or any of that process? Do you remember what you took with you?

ZEMANOVIC: My … mother came with one trunk [pauses], and I think we had also a smaller suitcase … for personal belongings or whatever. But in this trunk were—and I always marveled at what was considered her most valuable possession, was this feather, feather bed, feather [pauses] quilt, and feather pillows. Apparently that, that was what every potential wife who expected to get married had to bring … into the family as a dowry—her part of … the contribution to a newlywed, you see. She, the women were supposed to provide the, well, [pauses] pillows, and the quilts. And, of course, … the process of making these quilts was one of the projects in the evening … in these farmhouse lofts they had by lamplight in the evening, they would have these … goose down and goose feathers and duck feathers, and they would be peeling off the feathers from the quills, so that [they] … wouldn't be coarse or whatever else. And so that was always something that every woman and groups of women would get to do, and make these feather bedding.… And that's what … my mother brought with her in this trunk. I don't recall that she had anything else to contribute. She had this trunk and in there was this monstrous overstuffed quilt and the pillows. And I don't know just how many there were, but I think there were just two, and maybe more, because I remember sleeping under them.… I don't recall that she brought any … other material substance. We had the clothing, you know, for day-to-day clothing changes and whatever else, but I can't recall that there was anything else.…

SIGRIST: Saying good-bye to grandparents. Do you remember saying good-bye or your mother saying good-bye to them?

ZEMANOVIC: I vaguely remember that we were driven to the station in Trencin, which again was only a few kilometers away, because that's where my mother used to go and other family members used to go to the market to peddle whatever wares [they] might have had—farm produce or chickens or ducks or geese or whatever else. There … was no market in Dolna Suca. Anything that they wanted they had to go to Trencin, and that's where the railroad station was, and that's where we were driven to on our departure. But I don't really recall that there were, that I had any tearful farewells, or whatever else like that.…

It was all a blur, you might say.... Things were happening so fast, and I really didn't ... know that we were leaving, except in a vague way that we were going to join our father, OK? That much I recall, that we were going to meet our father....

SIGRIST: Do you have any impressions of seeing the boat for the first time and what you thought about that?

ZEMANOVIC: No. No, because of course you were moved along a gang-plank and right on. I do remember that we had a room in ... the lower part of the vessel. It was very hot and very noisy because we were apparently over the propeller shaft or whatever. That any time we were down there it was just thump, thump, thump, thump, thump. So ... it was very uncomfortable. It had [pauses] just enough room for my mother and my sister and me to sleep.... My mother, of course, along with everybody else, got seasick. She was seasick most of the time across the way.... My sister and I weren't seasick, and of course I had a ball on the vessel as far as I can recall. I climbed the mast, and I must have really driven the deck hands crazy, because one of the things that fascinated me—and I never got tired of watching for some reason—was ... at the aft end of the vessel, there was this huge section of gear with teeth in it and stuff. And it would move this way [he gestures], it would move this way, and it would move this way. And it was the steering mechanism. And I ... spent hours watching that thing for some reason.... There was not really much to do, you know, except run around on deck and try to keep from falling

overboard or whatever. And so as a six-year-old who wasn't seasick, I had ... the run of the main deck, of course, and we weren't permitted to go up into the other decks. They were reserved for the first-class and second-class passengers and whatever. And so ... we were fed down in the hold. I don't remember too much except ... one kind of a soup that I had never eaten ... before. And it was sort of like bro—it was cons—consommé. It had ... something that looked like—well, very small granular things floating around in it. It, well, you know, it was just something I had never eaten, because the soups we ate at home were real nice, thick hearty things, you know, that you could chew on. [He laughs.] And so this was something new to me....

SIGRIST: How long was the trip?

ZEMANOVIC: Ten days, I believe, is what it was. I think the trip lasted ten days, and I recall [pauses] as we started to approach shore, that we started to see birds. And we saw things floating in the water. I don't recall very much of the approach into the harbor, or anything like that, except we moved right along and [pauses] here we were.

SIGRIST: So [when] you arrived, was it July, you said?

ZEMANOVIC: We arrived August the first, August the second I believe is when we got here....

SIGRIST: Around that time?

ZEMANOVIC: Yeah. Yeah.

SIGRIST: Well, so you probably don't remember seeing the Statue of Liberty....

ZEMANOVIC: I wasn't aware of it. I don't know if anybody pointed it out or anything. But … it didn't leave an impression, let's put it that way.

DANES

Denmark is a small country in northern Europe, part of the area known as Scandinavia. Located on the Jutland Peninsula, Denmark covers 16,639 square miles and includes about 500 islands, 100 of which are inhabited. Denmark is made up of flatlands and gently rolling hills.

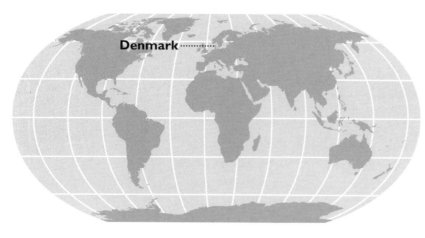

Denmark

Eighty-five percent of the 5,249,632 people who live in Denmark live in urban areas. Most residents are Scandinavian (Danish, Swedish, and Norwegian) or Eskimo. Danish is the official language of the country. Ninety-one percent of Denmark's people belong to the Evangelical Lutheran Church.

Denmark is a constitutional monarchy: a king or queen is the head of state, and the prime minister is the head of government. Denmark is divided into 14 counties; Copenhagen is the capital city.

Denmark is a highly industrialized country. Major industries include food processing, textiles, and electronics. Farming, fishing, and raising livestock are also important.

Danish Americans do not make up as large an ethnic group as do people from Norway and Sweden. Fewer people immigrated to the United States from Denmark than from the other Scandinavian countries because conditions were better in Denmark than in other parts of Europe. Danish immigrants settled over a wide area of the United States, unlike Swedish and Norwegian immigrants. Despite their relatively small numbers and rapid *assimilation* into (adaptation to) American society, Danish Americans have maintained their cultural heritage and become an important part of American life.

■ History

Archaeological research has found evidence of Danish settlements on the Jutland Peninsula and nearby islands in the Baltic Sea dating back to the 5th century. Several hundred years later the Danes were a major part of the Viking invasion of northern Europe and England. King Sweyn I conquered England in 1014. His son, Canute, was king of England (1016–1035) and Denmark (1018–1035).

During the late 12th and early 13th centuries, the Danes expanded eastward into the coastal areas along the Baltic Sea, where they established a powerful kingdom that was twice the size of present-day Denmark.

Danish power continued to grow during the late 14th century. In 1380 Denmark and Norway were united under King Olaf II, and after Olaf's death in 1387 his mother, Margaret I, ruled. In 1389 Margaret won the crown of Sweden and in 1397 created the Union of Kalmar, a political *confederation* (alliance) of Denmark, Norway, and Sweden, with Denmark as the dominant power. The Union of Kalmar lasted until 1523, when Sweden revolted and won its independence.

The 17th century saw several wars between Denmark and Sweden and between Denmark and Prussia. Denmark was badly defeated in the Swedish wars (1643–1645 and 1657–1660), when it lost several of its Baltic islands as well as all its territory on the Scandinavian Peninsula except Norway.

During the 18th century the Danes colonized Greenland, expanded their trade with the Far East, and established trading companies in the West Indies. However, during the Napoleonic Wars (1799–1815), when Napoléon Bonaparte tried to gain control of Europe for France, Denmark sided with Napoléon. After Napoléon's defeat in 1815, Denmark was forced to give Norway to Sweden.

◼ Coming to America

Compared with people from other ethnic groups, not many Danes have immigrated to the United States. Only one-seventh of the more than 2 million Scandinavian immigrants to the United States have been Danes, and fewer than 4 percent of the Danish people have immigrated to the United States.

Although the Danes are by far the smallest of the three Scandinavian immigrant groups, a great deal is known about the social background of early Danish immigrants. Between 1869 and 1914 Danish police recorded information about Danes who were immigrating to the United States. Registers contain the names of some 300,000 people as well as the year and month of each person's departure; the sex of each; whether he or she was traveling alone or in a group; and the person's occupation, age, place of last residence, and destination.

Very few Danes immigrated to the United States before the onset of the mass immigration in the mid-1800s. Those who did came to the colony of Dutch New Netherland (present-day New York State). The most prominent early immigrant to Dutch New Netherland was Jonas Bronck. In 1629 Bronck bought a large area of land north and east of Manhattan Island (now known as the Bronx) from the Native Americans.

Another famous Danish immigrant was a blacksmith from Copenhagen named Peter Lassen. Lassen blazed one of the early trails to California. The trail, along with a California mountain called Lassen Peak, was named for him.

In the late 18th and early 19th centuries, the Industrial Revolution, the

This 57-year-old Danish immigrant arrived in 1909 on the ship SS Mauretania.

Napoleonic Wars, and a rapid growth in population caused western European nations to suffer economic and social difficulties. However, economic and social conditions were better in Denmark than in the other countries, so few Danes immigrated to the United States during that period.

Conditions in Denmark declined during the 1860s. Defeated by Prussia and Austria in 1864, Denmark lost almost one-fourth of its territory and plunged into an economic depression. Meanwhile, continued population growth led to unemployment, crowded slums, a rising crime rate, and increased labor unrest.

A young boy in the garb of a Royal Danish Guard greets members of the Danish Royal Ballet at the unveiling of the statue of Hans Christian Andersen in New York City's Central Park.

At the same time, Danish citizens were hearing about opportunities in the United States. Letters from Danish-American pioneers appeared in newspapers. Rasmus Sorensen, a radical politician, urged all poor Danes to immigrate to the United States. Sorensen had immigrated to the United States in 1852 and settled in Wisconsin. He returned to Denmark to lecture

about the United States and to lead groups of Danes there.

After the 1870s agents hired by American railroad, steamship, and land companies began going to Denmark to encourage people to immigrate to the United States. Letters from friends and relatives in the United States also stimulated immigration, especially when the letters contained money orders or prepaid tickets. About 20 percent of all Danes who immigrated to the United States between 1868 and 1900 traveled on prepaid tickets. In addition, large sums of money were transferred from Danish families in the United States to relatives in Denmark via postal money orders. The money orders hit a peak of $2.4 million before the outbreak of World War I (1914–1918). However, how much of the money was used to finance immigration to the United States and how much was used to assist relatives who remained in Denmark is not known.

Among the large groups of Danes to immigrate to the United States in the 19th century were converts to Mormonism. Nearly 20,000 Danish Mormons immigrated to the Great Salt Lake area of Utah. They had learned about the Mormon religion and Utah's Mormon community from two missionaries who had traveled to Denmark from Salt Lake City in October 1849. Mormons were a religious minority in Denmark, where most people belonged to the Lutheran Church, a Protestant denomination.

Before 1900 about 56 percent of Danish immigrants were from rural areas. After 1900 about 52 percent were from cities and towns. Between 1868 and 1900, 55.5 percent of Danish immigrants were between 15 and 30 years old. Another 20 percent were children, and 22 percent were 30 years old or older. (The ages of the remaining 2.5 percent are unknown.)

Until about 1890 a high proportion of immigrants traveled in families. After 1890, however, the proportion of young single male immigrants rose, so many more men than women lived in the Danish communities in the United States. A Danish clergyman in the United States reported that he often heard complaints that Danish girls who had been brought to the United States to work for Danish families seldom stayed long with the families because they married Danish young men. He also reported that one employer had even specified that she wanted a servant who was "old and ugly," but even that servant was engaged to be married within six months.

Most Danish-Mormon immigration was family oriented. Figures from 1872 to 1894 show that among Danish Mormons who immigrated, women slightly outnumbered men, 32 percent to 29 percent; 39 percent were children.

Many Danish-Mormon converts were of relatively modest means. They were able to immigrate to America because of the Mormons' Perpetual Emigration Fund. From 1850 to 1887 the fund financed the passage to the United States of about 50,000 poor converts from all over Europe. Careful records were kept, and advances for passage were supposed to be repaid, but many were not. So there was never enough money in the fund to accommodate all who wanted to immigrate to the United States. In Denmark poor families who wanted to immigrate to the United States met once a year with a representative of the American Mormon Church to learn how many of them could leave in the year to come.

In the 1890s Scandinavian immigration shifted from a mostly rural to a mostly urban movement. A larger percentage of people from Danish towns and cities immigrated to the United States than did people from rural areas, although many of those leaving the towns and cities had moved there from the countryside.

Employment Opportunities for Women

The shortage of female Danish immigrants improved the labor market for young Danish women. A Danish politician who visited the United States in 1887 wrote the following in a Copenhagen paper:

The demand for Scandinavian girls, particularly Danish ones, is enormous. [A New York employment broker] told me that I was welcome to send 3,000 girls any day I pleased. Inside a few days he would promise to get them all work at a beginner's wage of 7 to 12 dollars. Girls who are skillful at housework and dairywork might obtain 25 dollars. Working in the fields is unknown for women in the States.

Few Danish immigrants were from upper- and middle-class families. Of the few who were, a number were sent to the United States by their families to avoid the shame of alcoholism, bankruptcy, or marriage beneath their station. Danish police provided some criminals and paupers with one-way tickets to the United States, but the total number of "undesirables" was very small. The vast majority of Danish immigrants were law-abiding peasants and working-class people. Between 1869 and 1900, 69 percent of adult wage earners who immigrated to the United States were laborers and servants, and more than 18 percent were craftspeople and artisans. After World War I, however, the proportion of educated and skilled workers grew steadily, and by World War II (1939–1945) they made up the largest group of Danish immigrants.

Few ethnic groups in the United States have been as widely and as thinly spread out as the Danes. Since 1870 they have been present in every American state and territory.

Danish settlements began to appear in the United States in the 1870s, when small groups settled in East Coast cities from Pennsylvania to Maine. Later arrivals often worked in businesses or factories run by earlier Danish immigrants.

Children in Elk Horn, Iowa, pose for their class photo in the early 1900s. At the time, Elk Horn had the largest rural Danish-American population in America.

In 1845 the first Danish farming settlement was founded near Hartland, Wisconsin. During the next two decades many more Danish settlements appeared in Wisconsin as well as in Illinois and Michigan. The early rural settlements were populated mainly by people who had come in organized groups from the same regions in Denmark.

In the peak years of immigration (1880–1920), the heartland of Danish America extended from southern Wisconsin across northern Illinois into Iowa. In the 1910 Census Iowa had the largest number of Danes—a little more than 10 percent of the Danish-American population. Wisconsin and Minnesota had the second and third largest populations of Danes.

Between 1886 and 1935, in an effort to preserve Danish ethnicity, Lutheran ministers and other cultural leaders cooperated with private land companies to develop nearly two dozen rural settlements in which land was sold only to Danes for a limited number of years. The settlements included Tyler, Minnesota (1886); Danevang, Texas (1894); and Solvang, California (1911).

Toward the end of the 19th century, Danish urban settlements began to grow rapidly. Three distinctly Danish neighborhoods existed in Chicago by 1889, although they had disappeared by World War II as Danes moved to the suburbs. Omaha, Nebraska; Racine, Wisconsin; and Council Bluffs, Iowa, also had major populations of Danes for many years.

■ Life in America

The change in the occupations of Danish immigrants after their arrival in the United States gives a clear picture of their upward mobility. The percentage of rural laborers fell sharply, and the percentage of landowners rose, indicating that large numbers of Danes achieved the goal of owning their own farms.

Although Danes entered a variety of occupations, they were most prominent in such fields as gardening, raising livestock, and dairy farming. Danish Americans soon became important in the American dairy industry and invented the most advanced equipment and developed the most advanced techniques in the field.

Perhaps the best-known Dane in the United States at that time was journalist Jacob Riis. An ardent reformer, he exposed the evils of New York City's slums through his articles, photographs, lectures, and books, such as *How the Other Half Lives* (1890). President Theodore Roosevelt called Riis "New York's most useful citizen."

Lutheran churches remained the central social organizations of Danish ethnic communities, and all Danish-American schools were church affiliated. However, Danes did not form as many ethnic religious institutions as did other Scandinavian groups.

Different attitudes toward assimilation into American society led to a split between Danish Lutherans in the United States. The conservative wing, commonly known as the Grundtvig faction, felt that Danes should settle together, establish Danish schools, and maintain their language. The Inner Mission wing of the church was opposed to attempts to foster Danish culture in America. As one of its leaders put it in 1888, "We should serve ourselves and our children poorly by doing all in our power to prevent them from becoming Americanized."

Because of their relatively low numbers and the fact that they were spread out across the United States, Danes assimilated very quickly into American life. Intermarriage with other groups was another reason for quick assimilation. According to the 1910 Census, 72 percent of American-born children of Swedish immigrants were children of parents who were both born in Sweden and only 57 percent of

American-born Danish children had both parents from Denmark. In addition, Danes who married outside their ethnic group had a greater tendency to marry non-Scandinavians than did either Norwegians or Swedes.

Danes also learned English more rapidly than did many other immigrant groups. A 1911 study of immigrants employed in mining and manufacturing reported that 97 percent of Danes spoke English, even though they had not been in the United States longer than other immigrant groups in the study. English is similar to Danish and so is easy for Danes to learn.

Several factors made Danes readily accepted into American life. They had a high rate of literacy, possessed a Protestant faith and work ethic, were familiar with the American political system, and were generally law-abiding. Such factors meant that Danish newcomers were not a threat to established Americans. On the contrary, they were welcomed wherever they went.

Danish immigrants who settled in Alden, Minnesota, sit for a family portrait.

Ellis Island Museum Oral History Project

NAME: Gerda Madsen Suttle
COUNTRY: Denmark
YEAR IMMIGRATED: 1914
AGE: 7 years
INTERVIEWER: Janet Levine

LEVINE: Do you remember anything that your mother packed to take with her to America?

SUTTLE: That vase … was the gift to my mother when I was born.

LEVINE: From whom?

SUTTLE: From Denmark.

LEVINE: Do you remember who gave it to her?

SUTTLE: No, I don't remember who gave it to her…. It has a few cracks in it, but it's probably quite valuable today, I imagine….

LEVINE: Maybe you could describe it for the tape, so somebody listening … could [know] what it looks like.

SUTTLE: Well, it's an orange vase with sort of small green leaves, and the base of it is sort of olive green. And there's a blue flower. I don't know what the flower is. It's a sort of blue with a white center. It's … really not a vase. What would you call it?

LEVINE: It's kind of an ornamental plant pot.

SUTTLE: Yeah. I think that's what you'd call it.

LEVINE: It's about maybe even a foot across in diameter at the top.

SUTTLE: Yeah.

LEVINE: So you've had that with you all these years.

SUTTLE: Yeah. Well, my mother had it…. She always had it in her living room; when she died I got that … and things like that.

LEVINE: Can you think of anything else your mother brought? Did she bring a lot of things?

SUTTLE: I really don't remember. Of course she brought our clothes. And we had beautiful clothes that was handmade all by her sister. She had four or five sisters too. And they all sewed for us. Beautiful clothes we had, you know.

LEVINE: Can you remember any of the clothes, maybe what you wore when you came….

SUTTLE: Yeah, I remember I had on a little blue sailor dress with a white collar. And patent leather shoes. And I remember this green coat I had. Green velvet coat. I remember just as plain as, it had little buttons in the front, a little collar, and a little green turban, you know….

LEVINE: So, then, did you bring that to America too?

SUTTLE: Yeah. And then my aunt had made me a … blue velvet dress. Not … velvet, just a blue dress. I forgot the material. But it was all embroidered on top with yellow, it was like yellow little flowers, and then the edge was scallop in yellow. She had done all that handwork herself. And I wore that a lot. In fact, I have a picture of that one my aunt did somewheres.

LEVINE: Oh, good. OK. Well, so you, did you bring any doll or anything that you had?…

SUTTLE: No. No, I don't remember. No.

LEVINE: Do you remember your farewells before you actually left?

SUTTLE: Not really. Just a little crying and hugging and tears, and that's all.

LEVINE: Did you think you would be coming back, or did you think you were?…

SUTTLE: I don't [know] what I thought. I was too excited. We were going to come to America, and it was something new.…

LEVINE: And the name of the boat?

SUTTLE: I think it was the White Star line.

LEVINE: And how about the passengers?

SUTTLE: Well, they [were] all seasick as I, far as I can remember. We all got seasick. And a lot of them were seasick. We were on the third class, which was the poor class. And I remember, oh, we could walk up,… and I would look in on the rich class with all their fruits and all their stuff. And I was jealous and envious to think that we couldn't have none of that stuff, because we had, oh, good food, but plain food. There was very much class distinction on the boat.

LEVINE: What…

SUTTLE: I don't even think the ones on the first class had to go [to] Ellis Island, if I remember right.

LEVINE: Right. You're right. That's correct.

SUTTLE: And it was just one and the third, maybe the second was tourist or something. I don't know, but we were down in the bottom.

LEVINE: Was there anything besides the food that showed this class distinction on this ship?

SUTTLE: Well, we really were not allowed up there, so I don't know. To just, you know, as a kid you sneak around. You try to get up the stairs, and up. And I was one of these I had to see everything, so every chance I could get and sneak away from the officer, up I ran. [They laugh.]

LEVINE: So, were you actually in the hold of the ship, in the kind of dormitory?

SUTTLE: Oh, no, we had a room.

LEVINE: You had a room?

SUTTLE: With four bunk beds. Small, but there was bunk beds on top and bottom.

LEVINE: So did your three sisters, brother, and mother…

SUTTLE: My brother was only three months old, so.

LEVINE: Oh. You were all in the same room.

SUTTLE: All in the same room.

LEVINE: And do you remember the food that you were served?

SUTTLE: No, I don't really remember the food. I think that they had a lot of fish, I remember. But we liked fish, so. It was just ordinary food.

DEPORTATION OF IMMIGRANTS

See ENTRY PROCEDURES; VOLUME 2: *ELLIS ISLAND: GATEWAY TO AMERICA*

DETENTION OF IMMIGRANTS

See ENTRY PROCEDURES; VOLUME 2: *ELLIS ISLAND: GATEWAY TO AMERICA*

DISCRIMINATION

See PREJUDICE AND DISCRIMINATION

DISEASES

See HEALTH PRACTICES

DISPLACED PERSONS

See REFUGEES

DUTCH

The Dutch people live in the Netherlands, a 16,033-square-mile country with 12 provinces, located in northwestern Europe on the North Sea. The land is flat and only about 37 feet above sea level. Much of the land below sea level has been drained and protected by about 1,500 miles of dikes. More than 3,400 miles of canals provide an important transportation system through the Netherlands.

The population of the Netherlands is about 15.5 million, 61 percent of whom live in urban areas. Thirty-four percent of the people are Roman Catholic, and 25 percent are Protestant.

Although the Dutch were one of the earliest groups to immigrate to the United States, they have not immigrated in great numbers. However, they have tended to settle in large clusters, giving them great visibility. Dutch immigration can be divided into three phases: (1) immigration caused by commercial expansion into America during the 17th century; (2) the mass immigration that occurred during the 19th and 20th centuries; and (3) the large number of refugees who came to the United States as a result of harsh conditions in the Netherlands after World War II (1939–1945).

■ History

The region that is now the Netherlands was conquered by Julius Caesar in 55 B.C., when it was inhabited by Celtic and Germanic tribes. During the 800s it was part of the empire of the great king Charlemagne.

After the fall of Charlemagne's empire, the Netherlands (then made up of Holland, Belgium, and Flanders) was split among a number of dukes, counts, and bishops. Eventually, it came under the control of Spain. In 1581 the Netherlands declared its independence as the United Dutch Republic. By the 17th century the Netherlands had become a major naval and economic power.

In 1815 the Congress of Vienna formed a kingdom of the Netherlands (including Belgium, which became independent in 1830). The Netherlands held many colonies around the world (including Indonesia, which became independent in 1949).

A Protestant denomination known as the Dutch Reformed Church became the national religion of the Netherlands during the 16th century. In 1834, however, several groups separated from the official church. Known as Afgescheidenen, or "Seceders," they opposed the way the government ran the Dutch Reformed Church. Church and government officials were alarmed by the threat to their authority, and many of the leaders of the Seceders were arrested, fined, and fired from their jobs. The persecution led to the immigration of 5,000 Seceders to the United States by 1850.

At the end of the 20th century the Netherlands has become a heavily industrialized country, although dairy farming and raising livestock are also important.

◼ Coming to America

The Dutch first came to America in 1609, when Henry Hudson explored what is now New York State in his ship the *Half Moon*. In 1614 the Dutch built a fur-trading post called Fort Nassau (later Fort Orange; eventually, Albany, New York). In 1624 this post became part of the Dutch West India Company's trading colony of New Netherland (present-day New York State), joined in 1626 by the settlement of New Amsterdam on Manhattan Island. By the time the English had taken control of New Netherland in 1664, the Dutch were a major presence there.

New Netherland attracted mainly religious refugees and poor immigrants, including Dutch soldiers, teenagers from Dutch poorhouses and orphanages, and farm laborers. Few families immigrated to America because of the dangerous ocean passage, the harsh wilderness, fears of attacks by natives, and the Dutch West India Company's policy of giving power to a few wealthy landholders, known as *patroons*.

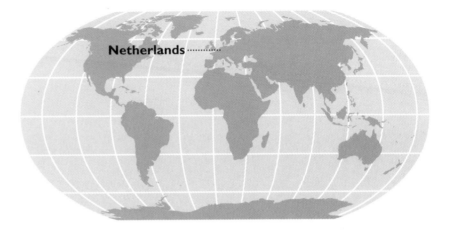

The English conquest of New Netherland in 1664 slowed the tide of Dutch immigration, but some Dutch continued to immigrate. The immigrants included working-class families, merchants who settled in American port cities, and Dutch Reformed Church clergy to serve the nearly 100 churches already established in America. Freedom of religion also lured Dutch immigrants to America. Several groups of Dutch Quakers and Mennonites joined William Penn's colony in what is now Pennsylvania.

Various conditions led to the immigration of 250,000 Dutch peasants and craftspeople and their families to America in the mid-19th century. Population growth in the Netherlands brought families seeking better economic conditions. During the mid-1840s a failure of the potato crop and a revolt against the Dutch Reformed Church caused a sharp rise in immigration. From 1845 to 1857 more than 20,000 people left the

Netherlands, including entire congregations of Roman Catholics and Seceders led by their pastors, or *dominies*. Jews from Amsterdam also immigrated during that time and settled mostly in New York City.

Dutch immigration continued to rise in the late 1800s. A crop failure in the northern Netherlands in the 1880s caused nearly 75,000 people to immigrate to the United States. Another 75,000 passed through Ellis Island between 1900 and 1914, and 35,000 Dutch arrived in the 1920s.

Dutch immigrants wait to be processed at Ellis Island around 1900.

In the late 1800s economic reasons motivated most Dutch immigration. Rising birth rates, rising living costs, periodic food shortages, plant and livestock diseases, and heavy taxes made American land and wage opportunities increasingly attractive. Letters from Dutch immigrants to friends and relatives in the homeland also motivated the Dutch to immigrate to the United States. Many of the letters appeared in Dutch newspapers—along with arguments from Dutch officials and

clergy, who viewed leaving their country as unpatriotic.

Lists compiled by the Dutch government show that the vast majority of immigrants were from rural areas. Farmers and day laborers made up 55 percent. Twenty percent were craftspeople, and fewer than 15 percent were professionals and businessmen. Many were poor—nearly 25 percent were listed as being "without means."

Some private and religious organizations, such as the Utrecht Christian Association for Emigration and the New York–based Netherlands Society for the Protection of Emigrants from Holland, helped Dutch immigrants. In general, however, relatives who had previously immigrated to the United States and Dutch-American church communities provided most of the assistance to newcomers. The "old" Dutch in the United States, who were prosperous and well established after many generations in America, had a strong religious and cultural identity with their homeland. They welcomed the new immigrants into their homes and churches and provided advice and financial assistance.

An improved Dutch economy and U.S. immigration quotas reduced the number of Dutch immigrants in the early 20th century. But Dutch immigration rose again after World War II left the Dutch economy so weak that the Netherlands could no longer provide for its people. The war had brought six years of Nazi occupation, heavy bombing, the murder of Dutch Jews, and the deportation of 500,000 workers to Germany. In the two decades after 1945 about 80,000 Dutch immigrated to the United States, including 17,000 displaced by a devastating flood in 1953.

By 1968, however, economic prosperity in the Netherlands had brought large-scale immigration to the United States to a halt. Fewer than 1,000 Dutch per year have immigrated to the United States since 1968.

The first Dutch immigrants to the United States settled near New York City. The 1790 Census reported that of the 100,000 people of Dutch origin living in the United States, 80,000 lived within 50 miles of New York City.

As farmland became scarce in the New York City area, young Dutch families moved north up the Hudson River and south into New Jersey. Others crossed the Delaware River into Pennsylvania. By the early 19th century Dutch farmers had pushed into western New York State and the Great Lakes region of the upper Midwest.

The 1840s saw the immigration of large religious and neighborhood groups. The groups settled primarily in the Midwest. Some 1,000 followers of Dominie Albertus C. Van Raalte founded a settlement called Holland in southwestern Michigan. Dominie Hendrik Pieter Scholte took his congregation of 900 to the prairies of central Iowa and founded the community of Pella. Father Theodorus Johannes Vanden Broek led 350 to the Fox River Valley of Wisconsin, where he created the largest Catholic Dutch colony in America, which grew to 40,000 people.

Those colonies and others like them soon spread into new areas. For example, by 1880 the Holland colony had expanded into five adjacent counties. By 1900 people from those areas had settled in the Upper Peninsula of Michigan as well as Detroit. As a result, the Dutch and their descendants are the largest ethnic group in western Michigan, numbering at least 150,000.

The Dutch also moved from rural areas to cities. Several Dutch communities near Milwaukee, for example, lost almost all their families to that city.

By 1880 the Grand Rapids (Michigan) furniture industry was largely Dutch owned. The Paterson (New Jersey) textile mills and the lumber mills in Michigan and Wisconsin also attracted a large number of Dutch workers. However, most urban Dutch preferred to remain independent. Some opened small shops that catered to Dutch customers; some worked as building contractors, laborers, and refuse haulers.

Later generations of Dutch immigrants moved into business, civil service, and professional occupations. As the cities became industrialized and densely populated, the Dutch moved out to the suburbs.

Nineteenth-century immigrants settled in self-contained neighborhoods, where they established formal and

Many Dutch immigrants settled in the Northeast. Here, two Pennsylvania Dutch children weed a garden while one rests in a wheelbarrow at a farm near New Castle in the Lackawannock township.

informal associations to maintain ethnic and religious ties. This was true in both rural communities and large cities. The Dutch community in the West Side of Chicago, for example, included Dutch-owned shops, professional offices, service businesses, a community newspaper, and even a Dutch section in one of the local cemeteries—identified by a decorative windmill. The community also had its own churches, schools (including a liberal arts college), and nursing homes.

These cousins of Dutch descent are experiencing their first Tulip Festival in Holland, Michigan.

■ Life in America

The center of the Dutch community was the church. The church leader was often the most important person in the community, serving as a real estate agent, banker, and politician as well as a spiritual leader. In later years, however, the church leader lost some of his power to lawyers and businesspeople.

Church life was also a key factor in preserving the Dutch language. In urban multiethnic Catholic parishes and Jewish communities, where immigrants mingled with people of other nationalities, the Dutch soon lost their language and culture. But the Dutch in the rural Midwest, who created isolated, church-oriented communities, generally retained their ethnic culture and the Dutch language for two or three generations. A strong community life and the arrival of new immigrants also encouraged the retention of the Dutch language and culture. However, after World War I (1914–1918), English made steady gains in Dutch churches, and by the 1960s few services were held in Dutch.

World War I was a turning point in Dutch Americans' *assimilation* (adaptation) into the American culture. People often confused them with Germans, and Dutch Americans fell victim to the prejudices of the time. Use of the Dutch language in Dutch schools and churches was called unpatriotic. A Dutch church and school building near Pella, Iowa, were burned, and the governor of Iowa issued a proclamation requiring the use of English at all public assemblies and in all churches and schools. War-generated feelings contributed to the quota system of the 1920s, which reduced immigration and cut off the support the Dutch community gained from new arrivals.

The Dutch have been politically active in the United States, although their small numbers and cultural isolation have limited their influence in national politics. However, the wealthy patroon families of the early Dutch colony—including families such as the Van Rensselaers, Schuylers, Roosevelts, and Stuyvesants—became quite well known on the state and national levels. Three U.S. presidents—Martin Van Buren, Theodore Roosevelt, and Franklin D. Roosevelt—were of colonial Dutch ancestry.

Today the Dutch keep their culture alive through annual folk festivals featuring traditional costumes, foods, and dances. Dutch language, history, literature, and culture are taught in many colleges throughout the United States. As a result, Dutch ethnic identity will likely survive.

Ellis Island Museum Oral History Project

NAME: Jessie Steinstra Eezmoneit
COUNTRY: Netherlands
YEAR IMMIGRATED: 1908
AGE: 10 years
INTERVIEWER: Janet Levine

LEVINE: And do you remember when it was decided that your mother and the children would be coming here?

EEZMONEIT: No. We came in September, I remember. But otherwise than that, no.

LEVINE: Do you remember leaving the …

EEZMONEIT: Oh, the children, my friends and all, oh, "We'll be back." And, of course, we never did. Some of my sisters went back. One of my sisters went back. One of my sisters went back about four times, another one about three times, another one once. I had no desire to go back.

LEVINE: Were you looking forward to coming? Do you remember going to …

EEZMONEIT: Oh, yes, oh, yes. We were, very much. I don't think my mother was. [She laughs.] She had to leave all her loved ones behind.

LEVINE: Do you remember anything about what you expected before you actually got here, or what you knew about America before you came?

EEZMONEIT: No, no. We did look forward to going, I think, because I remember my brother, he was just a little fellow, and he was always with my mother. And he'd say, "Mom, when are we going to America?" And she'd say, in Dutch, then, "Oh, when a ship with money comes over." And then … he'd say, "Mom, when is the ship with money coming over?" He was so anxious to get here, you know. He was just a little fellow. And there are certain things that stick out. And he was a cute little fellow.

LEVINE: Were there many people from your little town going to America at that time?

EEZMONEIT: No. There was a neighbor of ours that went on the same trip that we went. And we … came over on the *New Rotterdam,* which was … only its second voyage. And it took us nine days to come over, which was very, very quick. Because it was 1908, you know, and it was … a smooth trip, it was good. We had fog, I remember.

LEVINE: Do you remember leaving your home?

EEZMONEIT: Yes.

LEVINE: And what was that like, the actual departure?

EEZMONEIT: I believe it took us, I don't know how it was. They must have had a horse and wagon. They took us. And, no, an uncle of mine came. And he brought us over to, I guess the embarkment point was Rotterdam.

Hmm. But outside of that, I don't, I think my mother must have, it must have broken her heart to leave all her loved ones behind, but she knew what was best for the children. And she was always happy here. She said that she was glad she had come, and she was acclimated.

LEVINE: Did you have to wait in Rotterdam for any period of time?

EEZMONEIT: No, no.

LEVINE: Did you have any examinations?

EEZMONEIT: Oh, yes, indeed. Oh, yes, indeed. We had examinations as we entered the boat, and I think we had two on our way, and then another one when we came off the boat.

LEVINE: And … where were you? Were you in a cabin on the boat? Were you in …

EEZMONEIT: Yes, yes, yes, yes. Uh, I don't remember whether it was second or third class. I don't even remember that. But we were treated well, I know that, and the food was good.

LEVINE: Did you go to the dining room for food, or did the food, do you remember if you ate the food …

EEZMONEIT: I think we must have gone to the dining room, but I don't remember. I really don't.

LEVINE: Do you remember anything about the boat or the voyage?

EEZMONEIT: The trip, the people on the upper class seemed to take pity on my mother with all her children. And I had two sisters who were very, very winsome. And they treated … them so well. They would get up there, and they got things there that we wouldn't get

where we were. And there was a romance came out of that. Not my sister, a friend of hers. There was a man somewhere there that, I forgot what his position was in that upper class. And they finally got married and lived happily … in this country. Hmm.

LEVINE: So, after nine days the ship came into the New York harbor. Do you remember coming into the harbor?

EEZMONEIT: Yes, I remember, but believe it or not I don't remember the Statue of Liberty. But I remember very well, I remember my father saying, you know, we're sort of a slow nation. He says, "You … have to step on it a little bit." Getting on the trolleys and all. And everybody was in such a hurry. We just couldn't fathom that.

ECONOMIC EFFECTS

The economic story of American immigration is a story with two perspectives. On the one hand it is a story of individuals from all over the world who traveled to America in search of economic opportunity: good jobs and the day-to-day benefits of regular work. On the other hand it is a larger story of the effect the immigrants as a whole had on America's economic history over the years.

Historians and economists disagree on many aspects of the role immigration played in the economic life of America. Was immigration the cause of America's becoming the world's leading economic power? Or was immigration one of many contributing factors? Either way, an economic perspective on American history would be incomplete without addressing immigration. Immigration's role in the economic life of the country has also caused controversy and tension in American society. Periodically native-born Americans have felt threatened by the entrance of immigrants into the workforce. Those tensions, too, are an important part of the economic story of the United States.

Workers: The Basic Contribution

The basic way that immigration has contributed to the economy is by solving the problem of a lack of workers, or what economists call a *labor shortage.* The availability of large numbers of immigrants as workers has many results. A steady, reliable supply of workers helps businesses by decreasing the costs of production. A larger workforce not only produces more goods but can purchase, or *consume,* more as well. By increasing both productivity and consumption, immigrants have helped improve everyone's standard of living and helped the economy grow. Often entering the economy on the lowest rung of the ladder, immigrants generally have allowed the domestic workforce to move up and to advance into managerial or professional positions.

Native workers may feel threatened by large numbers of foreign workers, particularly when they are competing for the same jobs. And because poor immigrants will usually work for lower pay than native-born employees, the native workers fear a general fall in wages. In many instances, critics maintain, the immigrants' willingness to work for low wages—wages that are often far above normal for the land

from which they came—actually deprives native-born Americans of jobs. Such fears were expressed in numerous attempts to limit immigration in the late 19th and early 20th centuries, culminating in the passage of the Immigration Act of 1924. Although most scholars agree that immigration, on balance, has indeed been "good for America," complaints are heard increasingly that echo those of the anti-immigration nativists of the mid-19th century. Today critics of immigration argue that immigration has become a burden to the U.S. economy.

Workers crowd around a truck in California, hoping to be hired by the truck's driver for the day to landscape or do other jobs.

Building the American Economy

One way to measure immigration's impact on the American economy is by examining its effect on the nation's *gross national product,* or GNP. GNP is the total value of all goods and services produced by the residents of a nation during a year. Although GNP statistics are imprecise and open to different interpretations, they can provide a useful way to examine the strengths and weaknesses of an economy.

According to the *Harvard Encyclopedia of American Ethnic Groups* (1980), immigration has not significantly affected the rate of growth of GNP throughout the years. Rather, immigration has had an enormous effect on the total *size* of GNP, helping the United States develop the largest industrial economy in the world. America's rapid economic growth during industrialization (from approximately the mid–1800s to 1910) came mostly from advancements in industrial technology and efficiency. Well before the great immigration wave of the second half of the 19th century, America had already achieved its modern rate of GNP growth. That rate of growth was mirrored in the European countries that also underwent industrialization. However, since America was the recipient of so many immigrants, the total size of its economy grew far beyond the capacities of most European countries.

This 1916 photo of a 14-year-old girl working as a spool tender in a Massachusetts cotton mill led to the demand for an end to child labor abuses. In 1926 an amendment that granted Congress the power to regulate the labor of children under the age of 18 was proposed but never ratified. The Fair Labor Act, passed in 1938, states that no child younger than 16 may be employed in occupations involved in interstate commerce.

Colonial America to the Civil War

The connection between cheap labor and immigration was clear from the very first wave of immigration, which started with the colonists in the 1600s and reached its height just before the Revolutionary War (1775–1783). Colonial society was overwhelmingly agricultural, relying on preindustrial farming methods that involved hard, manual labor. Gradually the colonies developed the plantation system, which depended on growing and exporting such crops as rice and tobacco. To be profitable, the crops needed to be farmed on vast acreage with the help of a large, cheap workforce.

One way of securing such cheap labor was instituted by the Virginia Company. The Virginia Company—and eventually the British government—encouraged poor whites to travel to America as *indentured servants.* The immigrants signed a contract that required them to serve the company or another owner for a period of four to seven years in return for paid passage to the colonies. At the end of their contract period the immigrants gained not just their independence but also free land to farm. Despite the harsh treatment often given to indentured servants, there was enough immigrant interest in such an exchange to supply the South with its chief labor force during the 17th century. In addition, after they completed the term of their labor contracts, the indentured servants became independent members of society and became customers for colonial farmers and merchants.

Slavery

In their eagerness for extraordinarily cheap labor that would provide them with extreme profits, plantation owners quickly saw the economic advantage of indentured servants who would never gain their freedom. In order to secure cheap labor, plantation owners shifted from employing the willing participation of white indentured servants to exploiting the forced immigration of Africans as slaves.

The first Africans in America were 20 individuals who arrived in Jamestown in 1619 as indentured servants. By the 1660s colonial law had transformed all Africans into lifelong slaves. The steady growth in the number of slaves up until the Civil War (1861–1865) made the South's expansion of the cotton and tobacco industries possible. (One long-term effect of slavery was the creation of an underclass whose poverty is still an issue in contemporary America.)

Seeking to stem the tide of English workers leaving for America, the British government in 1662 gave the Royal African Slave Company the sole right to conduct the slave trade to America. The company provided African slaves to plantation owners in the South with the understanding that the slaves would never be freed. Slaves would have children, thereby guaranteeing a workforce whose labor costs would detract only slightly from the profits to be made in tobacco, rice, indigo, and other colonial products.

Despite the efforts of the British government, slavery in America took root slowly. In the 1650s African slaves made up less than 5 percent of the colonial population. By the 1770s, however, they constituted 22 percent of the total population, with much higher concentrations in the southern colonies of Virginia and South Carolina.

Northern colonies also relied on slave labor, but the proportion of slaves to general population was much lower than in the South, and slaves never became a central part of the economy in the North.

Although an extreme example, slavery demonstrates a pattern of behavior concerning the lengths large business owners would go to in exploiting immigrant masses for their own economic gain. The pattern has been repeated many times throughout American history, from underpaid and overworked coal miners of the Appalachian Mountains in the late 1800s to immigrant workers laboring under slave conditions in New York City sweatshops in the late 1900s.

The Civil War ended slavery in the South. It also represented the triumph of industrialization in the North over agriculture in the South.

At one time, children made up a third of the industrial labor force in the United States. The boys shown in this 1908 photo are working the midnight shift at an Indiana glassworks.

■ Industrialization and the "Great Wave"

Two centuries after the first Africans arrived in America a second wave of immigrants arrived to meet the labor needs of a developing industrialized America. Between 1820 and 1870 most of the 7 million immigrants who came to America were from northern and western Europe and settled in the Northeast and developing Midwest.

America's entry into the industrial age meant a need for workers in factories, which had started to dominate the economy of the northeastern and midwestern states. The need was met by a combination of European immigrants and freed African slaves who made their way north in a great migration to the cities. At the same time, the country was building a huge transportation network of roads, railways, and canals as it expanded westward. Cities in both the East and West saw the construction of new buildings, waterworks, sewers, and transit systems. The construction of such enormous projects was done almost entirely through the manual labor of unskilled immigrants. Without their efforts, the essential foundations of an industrial economy would not have been created.

By helping to lay the groundwork of a modern industrial society, immigrants sped up America's economic and territorial expansion. The movement westward, for example, was a by-product of the massive immigration of unskilled labor to the Northeast. Many native-born Americans who were unwilling to take the grueling jobs created by industrialization moved west. The factory, mine, and construction jobs they left behind were taken by immigrants. The immigrants continued industrial expansion, and native-born Americans continued to settle the frontier. As a vast labor resource, the immigrants enabled the mechanization of established industries and the development of new ones, including the railroad. They worked at the toughest, most dangerous, and lowest paying jobs to be found in cities.

In terms of total economic value, other figures besides the GNP reflect the stunning growth of the American economy during the years of industrialization. In 1860 total investment in U.S. industry approached $1 billion. By 1890 it had increased to $6.5 billion, and by 1910 it exceeded $13 billion. The industrial workforce jumped 300 percent between 1860 and 1890, with more than 8 million people working in factories, mines, and construction and transportation industries. By 1910 that number had almost doubled again. According to sociologist Leonard Dinnerstein, coauthor of *Natives and Strangers: A Multicultural History of Americans* (1996), the native birthrate and movement from farms to cities "simply could not provide the labor demanded by this fantastic economic explosion."

The enormous growth in the U.S. economy coincided with the third

Samuel Slater

Samuel Slater was one individual immigrant who played a crucial role in the beginnings of America's great industrial revolution. Slater was an expert in cotton manufacturing before immigrating to the United States from England in 1789 at the age of 21. At the time, British law forbade textile workers to immigrate and forbade the export of drawings of textile machinery. (A contemporary example of such a policy might be if the United States forbade the export of computer technology.) Once he reached America, Slater constructed versions of advanced textile machinery almost entirely from memory. In 1793 he established the first successful cotton mill in the United States. Beginning in Rhode Island, he founded a whole string of plants and even a town in that state that still bears his name, Slatersville. Slater's achievements, accomplished in spite of the opposition of the British government, paved the way for the development of the U.S. textile industry in the 19th and 20th centuries.

major wave of immigration to the United States. This influx of immigrants has become known as the "great wave." From 1881 to 1920 almost 23.5 million people streamed into the United States from almost every part of the world. Until the 1880s most immigrants came from northern and western Europe, but beginning in the 1890s, the majority of arrivals were people from southern and eastern Europe.

As Dinnerstein notes, the exploding industrialization and mass influx of people had greater economic benefits for the business owners than for the workers themselves. He cites as an example the Pullman Company, maker of railroad cars. In 1893 Pullman paid wages to workers totaling just over $7 million and profits paid to stockholders totaled $2.5 million. In the next year wages fell to only $4.5 million but profits increased to $2.9 million. According to Dinnerstein, such figures prove that workers were forced to suffer economic setbacks even as industrial owners maximized their profits.

Skilled Labor

Besides the unskilled laborers who provided the raw manual labor that fueled the industrial machine, skilled immigrants also contributed significantly to economic growth in the late 19th and early 20th centuries. In fact, at the beginning of industrialization many manufacturers recruited skilled immigrants right into their workforce, sometimes recruiting people before they had even immigrated to America. For example, English and Northern Irish handloom weavers put out of work by power looms in their homelands brought their experience directly to the mills of the

northeastern United States. And manufacturing profited from the know-how of German glassblowers and brewers, English textile workers, and Welsh coal miners.

The Germans and the Irish made up two-thirds of the second wave of immigration, significantly swelling the ranks of the workforce. The Germans, who settled in Pennsylvania and the states of the Midwest, tended to be successful at moving from being the lowest paid workers to being skilled tradespeople such as machinists, tailors, distillers, cabinetmakers, bakers, and butchers. They also contributed to the growth of the beer industry, which thrived in an area bounded by St. Louis, Missouri; Milwaukee, Wisconsin; and Cincinnati, Ohio. The area was often called the German Triangle. Like Scandinavians, the Germans often moved westward to acquire cheap—even free—land. They cultivated land that native-born Americans rejected and took the worst industrial jobs that Americans refused. The success of German immigrants in both the rural

A Mexican-American worker stitches dresses for a California women's clothing company.

and higher-level urban economies is evident: by 1870, 25 percent were employed as farmers and 37 percent as skilled workers.

Andrew Carnegie

Andrew Carnegie came to the United States the son of an impoverished textile worker and died one of the richest men in all America. Carnegie's story qualifies as the ideal realization of the immigrant dream, a dream that promises that through diligence and hard work one may find great success. During America's industrialization not only did Carnegie achieve great success, he also helped shape America's economic way of life.

Andrew Carnegie was born in Scotland in 1835. Like other Scots at the time, Carnegie's father suffered economic setbacks during the early years of industrialization. The elder Carnegie was put out of work, like so many textile workers, by the invention of the power loom, a device for manufacturing textile materials. Carnegie's family immigrated to the United States in 1848. The young Carnegie quickly proved his worth as personal secretary to an official of the Pennsylvania Railroad Company. Because of his own hard work, his insatiable ambition, and his phenomenal business sense, Carnegie succeeded at almost every industry he tried. His fame and fortune peaked in 1889 with the founding of the Carnegie Steel Company. He brought many manufacturing and management innovations to the steel industry, and it wasn't long before America was the worldwide leading steel producer. Carnegie enjoyed astronomical wealth and was reportedly worth about $500 million.

Carnegie is remembered as much for his charity giving as for the industries he created. In two works, *Wealth* (1889) and *Gospel of Wealth* (1900), he argued that rich men have a duty to use their surplus wealth for "the improvement of mankind." During his lifetime and through his foundations, Carnegie gave away nearly $350 million. The most visible example of Carnegie's legacy are the nearly 2,500 free public libraries he and his foundations have endowed throughout the United States.

Irish immigrants tended to be poor, particularly those who came in the late 1840s and early 1850s, when they fled their homeland because of a potato blight. They concentrated in the northeastern cities, lacking the money to buy farms or to prepare frontier land for agriculture. Instead they filled the bottom socioeconomic ranks, working as common laborers and household servants and sometimes landing in poorhouses, jails, and charity hospitals. In 1850 about 64 percent of Irish immigrants were employed as servants.

However, Irish immigrants also were strong participants in the labor movement and contributed tremendously to the growth of American labor rights. For example, in the 1880s Irish dockworkers in New York City and northern New Jersey pressured employers to yield to workers' demands for better working conditions by instituting a boycott of some of the goods handled by the port.

Excluding the Competition

As long as immigrants took jobs and opportunities rejected by native-born Americans, their presence was generally considered an asset. Even so, there were economic aspects to early 19th-century arguments to restrict immigration. As industrialization grew, the native-born American working class employees started to protect their interests against those of their employers. The formation of trade unions and other organizations was one move to gain better working conditions, higher wages, and greater job security. Industrialists opposed any such gain in workers' rights and power. By serving as a source of cheap labor, immigrants gave employers greater control in the conflict. Besides being willing to work for less than what their American counterparts considered a fair wage, immigrants eager for employment were often used by industrialists as *strikebreakers* (people hired to replace striking workers). In times of economic difficulty, when jobs became scarce, native-born Americans inevitably resented the foreign competition.

The case of Chinese immigrants in California in the 1850s illustrates all those issues. According to records, up until 1851 only 46 immigrants had come from China. But that changed rapidly later in the decade. Chinese escaping poverty, overcrowding, and the chaos of the Taiping Rebellion (1850–1864) took advantage of the cheap transportation between Hong Kong and San Francisco to settle in California. Initially they were welcomed as valuable workers for the many menial jobs in the new, little-populated state. They mined and cleared the land for agriculture. By 1860 they were a dominant force in the state's manufacture of clothing, shoes, tinware, and cigars. But the greatest demand for laborers from China came with the building of the transcontinental railroads in the 1860s. In fact, Chinese made up 90 percent of the labor force on the Central Pacific line; the Union Pacific line depended mostly on Irish workers.

Once the two railroads were completed in 1869 and approximately 10,000 Chinese workers flooded San Francisco, Californians began to feel threatened by competition. The animosity against the Chinese became national in the 1870s when shoe manufacturers in North Adams, Massachusetts, and laundry owners in Belleville, New Jersey, imported Chinese strikebreakers. As a result of the anti-Chinese immigration movement, unions began using a label on products to assure customers that white workers rather than Chinese workers had manufactured their products. The first label appeared in San Francisco in 1872 on cigars.

Racist attacks and physical violence against the Chinese preceded attempts to legislate against their presence. In 1882 America passed its first law limiting immigration—the Chinese Exclusion Act. Criticized as "the legalization of racial discrimination" by one politician at the time, the Chinese Exclusion Act effectively halted Chinese immigration into the United States. Immigration for most groups would not be limited until the passage of the Immigration Act of 1924. Although later periods of anti-immigrant fears would not lead as far as the Chinese Exclusion Act, similar bursts of anti-immigrant resentment based on economic fears would be a constant feature of the immigrant experience to the present day.

Samuel Gompers, a British immigrant, served as head of the American Federation of Labor.

▮ Trade Unions

Industry owners were attracted to immigrant labor because it was cheap. And immigrants had to fight fiercely for improvements in working conditions. The main vehicle for action from the immigrant workforce in America was the *labor union,* an organization of workers formed to advance the members' interests in terms of wages, benefits, and working conditions.

American trade unions are distinguished by their ethnic character. That is, the immigrant labor that made America's industrial boom possible formed the majority of trade unions. Although immigrants made up roughly 14 percent of the total American population during the great wave of immigration, they constituted nearly 25 percent of employees in transportation, nearly 36 percent of employees in manufacturing, and 45 percent of employees in mining. Immigrants made

The Molly Maguires

For the workers whose cheap labor provided the backbone of the industrial revolution, factory work was often hazardous and degrading. Unionization provided one means of fighting oppressive work conditions. Another means was the organization of secret groups who protested worker mistreatment using violent methods. In eastern Pennsylvania, coal miners formed one such secret society, the Molly Maguires. The group, active from 1843 to 1876, used terrorist tactics to threaten and allegedly kill mine bosses and to destroy coal trains, all in an effort to end the mistreatment of Irish workers in America. An undercover agent who had infiltrated the group and orchestrated the arrest of its leaders finally halted the Molly Maguires. Of those arrested 19 were hanged. Although the group was not a labor organization, it found many sympathizers among America's labor movement.

up nearly 58 percent of wage earners in the top 20 mining and manufacturing industries in 1909. Since the workforce was so overwhelmingly characterized in ethnic terms, it is no surprise that the labor movement was as well. The participants in trade unions—the rank-and-file workers as well as union leaders—were overwhelmingly European in origin, with a clear memory of unions in their homelands.

Local unions of workers of the same trade emerged fairly early in U.S. history, before 1800. The local unions were united by their common economic demands: suitable wages, decent labor standards, control of their own membership, and the right to strike. By the mid-1850s, as transportation and communication networks spread throughout the country, national labor unions began to replace local ones.

Unions faced numerous challenges in their quest to help their members. When the economy slowed, unions that had been cooperating to face big business together often split apart, concentrating instead on saving jobs in their own industries. Although ethnic bonds sometimes helped unions overcome challenges by persuading workers to work together, ethnic bonds often separated communities politically. A philosophy of "pure and simple unionism" helped overcome such political divisions by swearing off all direct political activity. That philosophy became dominant in America. "Pure and simple unionism" stressed narrow job concerns over widespread social reforms. According to Samuel Gompers, a British immigrant and American union leader in the late 19th and early 20th centuries, no matter what differences divided workers—race, creed, religion, or politics—all workers were united in the common purpose of maximizing their earnings and benefits. Although that approach succeeded in masking various ethnic differences, it failed miserably when it came to racial harmony, as black workers found themselves effectively shut out of union activities until well into the 20th century.

The discrimination against blacks was just one example of problems within unions. Eastern European immigrants, who began to arrive at the turn of the century, also found themselves discriminated against by unions. Often uneducated, unable to speak English, and unskilled, the immigrants were discriminated against even by people from the same country who had come to America only a generation or two before. The anti-immigrant stance on the part of organized labor can be seen in unions' support for ending America's open-door immigration policy in the 1920s.

From without, American unions faced fierce opposition from industry owners, who worked to retain complete control over their workers in order to keep profits as high as possible. Large businesses fought unionization in factories, hiring private guards and strikebreakers who often clashed violently with striking workers. The advances unions won for their workers often followed ferocious and bloody struggles.

Although never reaching the level of influence of unions in Europe, American unions have won important battles, from the implementation of the ten-hour workday in 1835 to wage increases, guaranteed vacation time, and workplace standards that are still in effect today.

■ The Case against Immigration

The last significant wave of immigration to the United States has occurred since World War II (1939–1945). America's industrial power, fueled by immigrant workers, proved itself in the immense effort to produce war materials during the fight against Germany and the Axis powers. Quotas that had been put in place restricting immigration in 1924 were relaxed to allow refugees from the war to enter the country. In 1965 the quotas were eliminated entirely. The effect has been an explosion of immigration that rivals the numbers produced in the great wave of immigration from 1880 to 1920. Instead of European nationals, however, immigrants from Asia and Latin America have dominated the latest wave.

The economic effect of the latest immigration has been a matter of some controversy. Although many of the latest immigrants have successfully adapted to the American economy by contributing to productivity and consumption, others have come to be viewed as a burden to society and as competitors to American workers. According to critics of immigration, many of the latest immigrants are stuck in a cycle of poverty and act as drains on public resources, consistently taking advantage of the *welfare system*—a system of public assistance put in place by President Lyndon Johnson in the mid-1960s. In addition, say critics, those who do work take jobs from native-born American

Scottish-born Andrew Carnegie, industrialist and philanthropist, developed the Pittsburgh iron and steel industries and used his wealth to endow libraries, schools, and other cultural institutions.

workers by their willingness to accept low wages and to tolerate poor working conditions.

Echoes of the anti-Chinese campaign of the 1870s and the continued prejudice against African Americans can be seen in some arguments against modern-day immigration. More careful critics, however, strive to make reasoned economic arguments for limiting immigration into the United States.

In *The Case against Immigration* (1996) Roy Beck argues that "immigration turns out to be a perverse federal Robin Hood scheme that takes from middle-class workers and gives to the country's most affluent." The continuing influx of immigrants allows industry to slash pay and demand more work, to the detriment of workers' well-being but to the benefit of corporate stockholders. According to Beck, business owners have conspired to make jobs unattractive to most Americans in order to hike profits by exploiting the

low expectations of new immigrants. And although such workers are "cheap" to the businesses that employ them, they carry high costs for the communities in which they reside. Among the costs are those for social services and education for immigrants and the costs for social services provided to displaced native-born American workers.

In addition, says Beck, the unchecked influx of new immigrants places a severe burden on the public school system, which educates the children of immigrants whose poverty prevents them from paying for their share of the schooling. According to Beck, this situation is unfair not only to Americans but also to the immigrants, who by being allowed into the country may be given a false hope that they can expect to escape their poverty.

■ Economics of Illegal Immigration

In the modern period of immigration (1960s to present) work by illegal aliens has become an important factor in the U.S. labor market. Currently, anywhere from 3 million to 6 million illegal immigrants reside in the United States. Most of the illegal immigrant workers are from Mexico and have become part of America's *secondary labor market*. The secondary market includes low-paying, menial jobs, which are often temporary but are necessary to the proper functioning of the economy. The workers in the market include farmworkers, dishwashers, laborers, garbage collectors, building cleaners, restaurant employees, gardeners, and maintenance workers. The native-born Americans who are willing to take those jobs are either shut out of the jobs by illegal immigrants, who will work for

---

Proposition 187

Proposition 187 was a ballot initiative voted on by the people of California in 1994. It was an effort by concerned Californians to deny public services (such as schooling and emergency health care) to immigrants who were in the state illegally. State officials had put the costs of the services at more than $2.5 billion. The measure passed 59 percent to 41 percent, but parts of it were soon declared unconstitutional.

Proposition 187 generated intense public discussion of the pros and cons of illegal and legal immigration to the United States. In a related policy move, President Bill Clinton decided to stop giving Cuban boat people special status as political refugees, which they had been given following the Mariel boat lift of 1980. This change in status meant that instead of being allowed into the United States, Cuban boat people would be returned to Cuba. Both for Cubans seeking to come to Florida and Mexicans and other Latin Americans wanting to come to California, anti-immigrant sentiments have made it harder than ever to achieve the American dream.

less, or are forced to work for lower wages themselves. The supply of illegal immigrant labor, especially in the border states of Texas and California, acts to keep down wages that would be expected to rise.

Often employers prefer to hire illegal immigrants because their illegal status makes them easier to manipulate than American citizens. An employer can always threaten to turn an illegal immigrant in to the authorities if the illegal worker will not do exactly as the employer wishes.

The U.S. government sought to overcome some of the problems associated with illegal immigration with the Immigration Reform Act of 1986. A central piece of the legislation was granting *amnesty* (pardon) to all illegal immigrants who could prove they had been living in the United States continuously since December 31, 1981. Nearly 3.1 million people were accepted into this program. However, other provisions of the legislation did little to stem the tide of illegal immigration into the United States, particularly from Mexico. For example, although employers were required to verify the eligibility of all employees, agricultural businesses in Texas and California were granted exemptions that made it possible for them to still hire seasonal laborers who were in the United States illegally. Despite tough language on shutting down the border, the 1986 act in effect provided expanded legal methods for the importation of more farmworkers.

◼ Immigrants' Effect on the Economy

Since the start of the colonial period more than 60 million immigrants have come to America. As a whole the immigrants found the opportunity to fulfill the dream of economic security that had driven many to come to America in the first place. In immigrating, they contributed mightily to the economic growth of the United States, a growth that has made the United States the leading economic power in the world. Although many Americans today wonder about the economic consequences of continued immigration, it is clear that immigrants will continue to play an important role in America's economic life.

Ellis Island Museum Oral History Project

NAME: Jack Levine
COUNTRY: Russia
YEAR IMMIGRATED: 1913
AGE: 20 years
INTERVIEWER: Paul E. Sigrist Jr.

…

LEVINE: I walked with my brother in the street, and we used to go into the park every day. There were always people in the park talking, talking about trades and the unions. My brother meets a friend and says, "This is my brother who just came from Europe. He's looking for a job. He has no trade. He can fake any job." The friend says, "I work in a shop where we're making garments, rainwear." We made a date, and he takes me to the shop, a small shop, with about ten people working on sewing machines. And I see an empty sewing machine. So I ask to see the boss. He takes me to the boss, who says, "We haven't got too much work." My friend says, "But he just came in from Europe, and he needs a job and he can learn to do something." The boss says, "I'll take him, provided one of the machine operators can teach him how to do it." My friend says, "Near me is an empty machine, so I can show him." They took me in and my friend puts me at the sewing machine and tells me how to use it, how to put cotton in it, how to use the shuttle, everything. He gave me little pieces of cloth, rags, and showed me how the machine sews. And he saw to it that I was doing it all right. After a week, the boss gives me $5 and says, "Never thought you could do it, but you're worth $5." Three weeks later, a man comes into the shop, and he is from the Ladies Garment Workers Union. He came up and said to the boss, "I want to talk to your workers." So the boss stops the power so that all the machines stop. The man starts to talk. For me it was something new. The man said to us, "You are working long hours. You are worth more than your boss thinks you are worth. You work with your hands, but it's your boss who decides how much money you should get." And one worker stands up and says, "We will become union people," and he went down and registered. It cost $4. Everybody paid. For $4 you became a union member. I was working there for five months until the work went slack and no more orders came in. Later I made ladies' skirts and blouses, and when the First World War [1914–1918] broke out, I made leggings for the Army. Then there was no slack. We worked all year, making $11 or $12 a week.

Ellis Island Museum Oral History Project

NAME: Emma Schmid Schwarz
COUNTRY: Germany
YEAR IMMIGRATED: 1926
AGE: 18 years
INTERVIEWER: Paul E. Sigrist Jr.

…

SCHWARZ: The next morning after I arrived, I was taken to get a job. And a lady liked me and said she would pay me $14 a week. And on the next morning, I went to the home where I would be working. Just one day and I was working! I was hired as a domestic. I had my own room up on the third floor. The family had three children, and I had to cook and take care of the household. They had someone else who came in to do the cleaning. I couldn't speak a word of English, and the lady [who] hired me couldn't speak German. So she had a German-English dictionary, and she'd go around with me…. She'd hold the glass and say, "Glass," or the forks or spoons or plates. She'd always be so patient with me. She taught me all these things, and in the evening, at first, she'd help me with the cooking. I also had to serve during dinner. She taught me about where to put the fork, the soup spoon, the smaller fork, just how the table had to be set. During dinner, her husband would sit at one end of the table and no matter what kind of food they were having, he would serve [it] onto the plates and I had to serve it to the people around the table. I remember one Sunday we had a big roast beef. When dinner was ready, I brought the roast out and placed it in front of her husband. He had the plates, and he carved this roast and put it on the plates. By the third slice, blood started running out of the roast and, oh my God, I had never seen a rare roast in my life. In Germany, we cooked everything well done. They said I just passed out. They carried me onto a couch, and when I woke up, I was in my bed on the third floor. And all I could think was, "I will be fired. I will lose my job, and then what will I do?" But nothing was ever said. I can't tell you the feeling when you don't understand things. You stand there like a real dummy. You try so hard to listen to every word. The children's playroom was near my bedroom on the third floor. When the children weren't there, I tried to read all the first-grade, second-grade, third-grade books they had. Every spare moment that I had I would go through the books, and that's how I learned to get along at first.

SEE ALSO: Forced Immigration; Illegal Immigrants; Immigration Law and Policy; Living Conditions

EDUCATION

Throughout the 1800s hundreds of thousands of immigrants entered the United States. Some spoke foreign languages; some had different religions; all came from different cultures. Public education was an important factor in the *assimilation* (adaptation) of the immigrants and their children to American life. It helped them fit in and function in their new culture. As the ethnic makeup of the United States changed, especially in the big cities, many people came to believe that public schools were the ideal places for immigrants to learn English, the customs and traditions of their new land, and the principles of democracy. Education became one of the major forces in "Americanizing" the new arrivals.

Before the 1800s education in America was the responsibility of a child's family or community. Most children were taught reading, writing, and the skills they would need as adults at home. In some cases communities were charged with educating children. In 1647, for example, the Massachusetts Bay Colony passed a law requiring that every town with more than 50 households establish a primary school.

The public school movement began in the 1830s, led by a Massachusetts politician and reformer named Horace Mann. Mann believed that all children, rich or poor, should have access to state-regulated, tax-supported education. Mann had many opponents: some

A group of immigrants learn English to prepare for the language portion of the naturalization test in Nogales, Arizona, in 1997.

people didn't want tax money spent on education; others were afraid that public schooling would reduce the amount of available child labor. However, support for Mann and his "common schools" grew. Soon graded schools appeared across the country, along with teacher training and certification schools. By the early 1900s all states had compulsory education laws that required children to attend school, whether public or private.

Not all immigrant groups shared the same views on the importance of formal education. Some groups, such as the Jews, came from a culture that placed a high value on learning. Even before compulsory education laws, Jewish immigrants took advantage of the free public schools as well as public libraries and free lectures.

Vietnamese-American students in San Jose, California, listen to a lesson in their English as a Second Language (ESL) class in 1995.

Other groups did not highly value formal education. Such groups as the Italians and the Irish placed an emphasis on skills and practical knowledge. Because a child's earnings were often an important part of an immigrant family's income, a child from an Italian family who chose school over work was seen as letting the family down. Children of Italian immigrants were expected to help support their families.

■ The Public School "Melting Pot"

More than any other institution, public schools were held responsible for Americanizing the children of immigrants. Reformers in the 1800s believed that the schools were the best places to unite the many groups of newly arrived immigrants by teaching them the "correct" values and customs and molding them into "Americans."

Teachers in big city public schools often found themselves teaching large classes of more than 60 students, crammed three to a desk in some cases. Some teachers found teaching immigrant children frustrating—especially those children who didn't speak English. Many teachers complained that immigrant children were lacking in manners and cleanliness and were often too tired from working after school to learn.

Immigrant children faced discrimination and prejudice not only from their teachers and native-born American classmates but also from their textbooks. Textbooks of the day were filled with stereotypes of groups that were different from the white Anglo-Saxon Protestant majority. Such stereotypes often caused a sense of inferiority and self-doubt in immigrant children.

As immigrant children were immersed in American culture, a rift between the generations often resulted. As some children became more "American," they learned to be ashamed of their parents and the ways of the old country. A survey of Polish immigrants and their children conducted in Buffalo, New York, between 1926 and 1928 found that some children were angry with their parents for refusing to Americanize. Their parents were also unhappy; many felt they were losing their children.

Not everyone agreed that public schools should be centers for Americanization. Jane Addams, the founder of Hull House (a *settlement house,* or 19th-century community center, in Chicago), was one of many people who recognized that public education caused problems between the generations and sometimes resulted in a loss of self-respect in immigrant children. Although Addams believed in helping immigrants assimilate, she and other settlement house workers felt that the assimilation should be gradual and that schools should not focus on erasing immigrants' cultures.

In places where there were large immigrant populations, school systems made an effort to retain some of the old cultures. Holidays, customs, and even the languages of the old cultures were preserved in the public school. In California in the mid-1800s, for example, immigrant children were taught in their native Spanish tongue. In the Midwest, where there was a large German population, many classes were taught in German; in Cincinnati, Ohio, children in first grade through fourth grade could attend classes in both English and German.

At the beginning of the 20th century the move toward Americanization heated up as World War I (1914–1918) loomed on the horizon. Fifteen states—many with large German populations—passed laws making English the only language used in public and private elementary schools. Identifying with any culture other than the American culture became unpopular and sometimes dangerous. In 1918, four months before the end of the war, former President Theodore Roosevelt stated, "There can be no fifty-fifty Americanism in this country. There is room here for only 100 percent Americanism, only for those who are Americans and nothing else."

Archbishop John Hughes

John Joseph Hughes immigrated to the United States from Ireland in 1816 with his family. In 1826 Hughes became a priest in the Roman Catholic Church. He was first assigned to the diocese of Philadelphia; in 1838 he became the bishop of New York.

A colorful, combative character, Bishop Hughes was not afraid to take on anti-Catholicism in any form. He wrote angry letters to newspaper editors who printed anti-Catholic articles, debated Protestant ministers, and fought to have anti-Catholic materials removed from New York's public schools. He also lobbied, unsuccessfully, for state funding for a separate parochial school system.

Nicknamed "Dagger John" for the shape of the cross that he always signed by his name, Hughes became New York's first Roman Catholic archbishop in 1850. Eight years later he laid the cornerstone for St. Patrick's Cathedral in New York City. Hughes also helped found Fordham University. He died in 1864.

Americanization through education wasn't aimed solely at the children of immigrants; adults were also targeted. Adult immigrants who needed instruction in English or help preparing for their citizenship tests could attend night school in most cities. Such classes, which taught English, history, laws, hygiene, and job skills, were initially sponsored by immigrant aid groups and other civic organizations. "Learn the language of your children," trumpeted one poster printed in Yiddish.

In the 1880s New York City school districts began offering night classes for adult immigrants; by the turn of the century tens of thousands of adult immigrants attended the classes. Even more people attended the so-called Americanization classes after New York passed a law requiring immigrants ages 16 through 21 who were not literate in English to attend school part-time. This type of law was passed in other states as well. Henry Ford, inventor of the automobile, required his non-English-speaking factory workers to take classes after working hours.

An English teacher in New York City explains the importance of the Fourth of July to recent Russian immigrants in 1990.

Alternatives to Public Schooling

Although some groups, such as the Jews, moved to have anti-Semitic and other offensive images removed from textbooks, others felt that more needed to be done. Catholic priests in particular worried that Protestant ideals were being taught to Catholic children. Parishes began setting up Catholic schools for children in order to preserve their religious identity.

In 1840 Bishop John Hughes of the diocese of New York petitioned the state for funds to set up a separate school system for Catholic children. (See "Archbishop John Hughes" sidebar on page 81.) Although the petition was denied, Hughes persisted. Many parishes in New York set up *parochial* (parish-run) schools for their children with their own funds.

As more and more states passed compulsory education laws, the number of parochial schools grew dramatically. In addition to a strong religious identity, parochial schools of the 1800s had strong ethnic identities. Catholic parents in Irish, German, French-Canadian, Polish, and other ethnic communities founded parochial schools in order to maintain the cultures of the Old World.

Because of strong ethnic ties, parochial schools were often attacked as not promoting Americanization. In the 1850s the Public School Society, Bishop Hughes's chief foe, stated, "When foreigners are in the habit of congregating together they retain their national customs, prejudices, and feelings," which, the society believed, made them "not as good members of society as they would otherwise be."

Despite the criticism, parochial schools stayed open, providing an alternative for parents who were unhappy with the public school curriculum. Today parochial schools are defined by their religious, not ethnic, affiliation.

Educational Exclusion

By the early 1900s free public schooling was available to all white immigrant children, even though some immigrant groups weren't entirely happy with the quality of that education. Nonwhites, however, were regularly excluded from a free education.

Blacks were among the people discriminated against most. Before the Emancipation Proclamation freed them, most black slaves had received little education. Most states in the South had laws against teaching slaves to read or write. As the friction between the North and South grew, many states in the South became even stricter, making it a crime for anyone to teach a black person.

Free black children in the North did not have access to the public education system. They were either excluded from public schools or were sent to *segregated,* or separate, schools. The segregated schools were generally inferior and poorly funded compared with the public schools for white children. In 1850, 11 years before the beginning of the Civil War (1861–1865), Massachusetts courts set the legal precedent for laws that came to be known as Jim Crow laws by ruling that separate but equal school facilities were legal. (Jim Crow laws, named for a stereotyped black character who appeared in a post–Civil War minstrel show, were laws that created separate social systems for blacks and whites in the South.) The ruling was overturned five years later, but racism and discrimination against black people continued in the North. As a result of this atmosphere, volunteer societies in the North opened their own schools to educate black children and provide job training for black adults.

After the Civil War the 13th Amendment to the U.S. Constitution was passed, prohibiting slavery and racial discrimination. Blacks in the South could now vote, hold elected positions,

and attend school. Hundreds of members of the American Missionary Association, a religious organization that grew out of the *abolition movement,* headed to the South, establishing 1,000 schools for black children within ten years. (The abolition movement was a reform movement started in the early 1800s that worked to rid the United States of slavery.)

During the post–Civil War period, racial tensions flared as many states passed "black codes" that effectively curbed the rights of blacks. The codes even allowed for black children to be "apprenticed" to former slave owners if their parents were found to be "unfit." Although the 14th Amendment, ratified in 1868, outlawed those discriminatory regulations, the situation for blacks in the South continued to deteriorate.

In 1896 legal discrimination against blacks was approved by the U.S. Supreme Court in *Plessy v. Ferguson.* The Court ruled that blacks were "separate but equal," making segregation the law of the land. Blacks could now

Elizabeth Eckford is turned away from Central High School in Little Rock, Arkansas, by members of the Arkansas National Guard on September 4, 1957. The guardsmen were instructed by Governor Orval Faubus not to allow nine black students, known as the Little Rock Nine, into the school.

be legally excluded from or segregated in white schools, theaters, restaurants, buses, trains, and most other public places. As long as the services provided to blacks were "equal" to those for whites, no law had been broken.

School facilities for blacks were not equal, however. Especially in the South, funds were diverted from black schools to the white schools. When money ran out, black schools, which were often overcrowded and falling apart, were the first to be closed. Rural black children who lived far from their schools were not given access to buses, unlike rural white children in the same situation.

The Little Rock Nine gather on the steps of Central High School in Little Rock, Arkansas, with President Bill Clinton and other officials in September 1997. The meeting marked the 40th anniversary of the school's desegregation.

Blacks worked to overcome this unfair system of education by pushing for integrated schools or seeking more funding for segregated schools. However, legal discrimination against black schoolchildren continued until 1954, when the U.S. Supreme Court decided *Brown v. Board of Education.* The case is considered one of the most important cases in the Court's history. It started in the early 1950s when the

father of a Topeka (Kansas) student brought suit against the city's board of education. Instead of attending a white elementary school just four blocks away from her home, Linda Brown, a seven-year-old black third grader, had to walk 20 blocks to the nearest black elementary school. Brown was denied admission to the white school because of her race.

When deciding *Brown v. Board of Education,* the Supreme Court ruled for Brown, stating that "separate education facilities are inherently unequal." The Court also stated that segregated schools violated the 14th Amendment. Chief Justice Earl Warren wrote that segregating children in school "generates a feeling of inferiority as to their status in the community that may affect their hearts and minds in a way unlikely ever to be undone." Although many school districts—especially in the South—found ways to defy the decision, *Brown v. Board of Education* was an education and civil rights milestone. (See "The Little Rock Nine" sidebar.)

◼ Exclusion of Other Groups

Blacks were not the only group of nonwhite Americans to be excluded from public schooling. Native Americans were also deprived of equal education.

Before the 1870s most treaties between the U.S. government and individual tribes promised federally funded education, job training, and other benefits to the tribes. In the 1870s the focus of Native-American education changed. Schooling was seen as a way to Americanize Native-American children, severing tribal loyalties and promoting "American" culture and values. Soon

"English-only" government schools replaced bilingual schools run by missions or tribes. Conditions in most of the schools were terrible and usually marked by strict discipline. Children who continued wearing tribal clothing and speaking their tribal languages often were severely punished.

Some parents refused to send their children into such an environment, but in 1893 Congress effectively forced the children to go to government-run schools by withholding federal support to families who wouldn't send their children. Those students who tried to attend white public schools in their area were usually turned away. In the 1930s the federal government began giving funds to states that admitted Native-American children into their public schools. Attendance in the government-run schools declined, and public school attendance rose.

Asian immigrants—especially those from China and Japan—also suffered from educational exclusion. In the late 1800s many people felt that Asian immigrants were not able to assimilate

The Little Rock Nine

Despite the U.S. Supreme Court's decision against segregation in *Brown v. Board of Education*, some school districts in the South looked for ways to sidestep the ruling. One such school district was the Little Rock (Arkansas) school district. For three years the Little Rock school board worked on a plan to integrate the public schools, finally deciding to allow a limited number of African-American students to attend the all-white Central High School.

Before the fall of 1957 more than 75 African-American students applied for admission to Central High. Only nine were accepted. The number was still too high for Arkansas Governor Orval Faubus. Before school opened, he warned that "blood will run in the streets" and announced that he was sending the Arkansas National Guard to Central High to prevent the African-American students from entering the school. On September 4 the nine students arrived at Central High for their first day of classes. As she tried to enter, student Elizabeth Eckford was spat upon and threatened by the angry mob that had gathered. The African-American students were turned away.

A federal court order forced Faubus to withdraw the National Guard, and on September 23 the "Little Rock Nine" attended their first morning of classes. Inside they were spat upon, tripped, and terrorized by white students. A crowd broke through barricades set up around the school and began looking for the African-American students. The Little Rock Nine made it out of the school safely.

Two days later the African-American students returned, this time under escort of the 101st Airborne Division. The soldiers, ordered to Little Rock by President Dwight D. Eisenhower, stood guard in front of the school and escorted the African-American students to their classes. Despite the armed guards, the nine students were mentally and physically tormented by their classmates. The students were beaten up, cursed at, spat upon—one of the students even had acid sprayed in her eyes with a squirt gun. Their families didn't escape unscathed either. Some lost their jobs for sending their children to Central High.

In February one of the nine students was expelled for fighting. Signs with the words *One Down, Eight To Go!* were posted throughout the school. But the other eight students didn't go—they completed the school year. The only senior of the group, Ernest Green, graduated. Dr. Martin Luther King Jr. was Green's guest at the graduation ceremony.

The following year, however, the remaining seven were unable to return to Central High. Faubus had shut down Little Rock's public high schools to prevent further integration. In 1960 Central High reopened, with just two African-American students enrolled. Both had been members of the Little Rock Nine. It was not until 1972 that all grades in Little Rock's public schools were integrated.

and become American. This attitude was especially strong on the West Coast, where the largest number of Asian immigrants had settled. In the 1870s and 1880s the city of San Francisco excluded Chinese children from its public school system. Although California law banned this kind of exclusion, in 1885 Asian students were still segregated from white students. Over time Asian immigrants began to assimilate and learn English, and public hostility toward them lessened. Asian students were eventually able to fully benefit from public school systems.

Kindergarten in the United States

The concept of a structured preschool education for young children was developed in 1837 in Germany by educator Friedrich Wilhelm August Froebel. Froebel named his programs *kindergartens*—a combination of the German words *kinder* (children) and *garten* (garden). His aim was to help young children understand the world around them through arts, crafts, games, and songs.

German immigrants brought kindergarten to the United States. Mrs. Carl Schurz, a German immigrant who had studied with Froebel, started the first U.S. kindergarten in 1856 in Watertown, Wisconsin. Schurz taught a group of German-speaking children in her home.

The English-speaking population soon adopted the kindergarten concept. In 1873 St. Louis, Missouri, became the first public school system to offer a kindergarten program. *Settlement houses* (community centers) also offered kindergarten programs. By the 1880s more than 400 kindergartens were operating around the nation. In 1900 kindergarten was an accepted part of public schooling.

Spanish-speaking groups, although legally considered white, also suffered discrimination and prejudice. In Texas the schools Spanish children attended were inferior to those attended by white students. Funds intended for the schools were often sent instead to white schools. Students were not allowed to speak Spanish on school grounds—a rule other states put into effect as well. In some areas of Texas "Spanish detention," being kept after school for speaking Spanish, was a punishment that continued into the 1960s.

In California Spanish-speaking children were segregated from English-speaking students on the basis of "need"—IQ tests were deliberately misinterpreted to suggest that Spanish-speaking children were intellectually inferior. By the 1930s these "findings" had been disproved, and in 1947 California declared segregation of Spanish-speaking students illegal.

■ Immigrant Education Today

Over the past few decades the battle between some school systems and immigrant groups trying to secure equal educational opportunities has continued. One example is the fight over whether the children of *undocumented* (illegal) immigrants should be allowed public education.

In the 1970s the Texas Education Code barred using state money to educate children who were not U.S. citizens or documented immigrants. The code allowed public schools to either turn away undocumented immigrants or charge them tuition ($1,000 per year in 1977). The 1982 U.S. Supreme Court decision in *Plyler v. Doe* ended that practice across the nation, striking down a Texas law that excluded undocumented immigrants from public education and giving *all* children the right to free public education.

The late 1990s has seen a return of anti-immigrant sentiment, especially in states where illegal immigrants enter the country. In 1994 California voters approved Proposition 187, which barred children of undocumented immigrants from attending public schools and receiving other state-funded services. (See "Proposition 187" sidebar on page 76.) Arizona, Florida, and Washington also tried to pass similar measures. In 1998 all elements of Proposition 187 were declared unconstitutional, based in part on *Plyler v. Doe.*

Plyler v. Doe has itself come under attack recently. In 1996 the U.S. House of Representatives passed the Gallegly Amendment, which would have allowed states to exclude undocumented immigrants from public schools. The amendment would have affected hundreds of thousands of children by effectively overturning the Supreme Court's 1982 decision. However, the Senate did not consider the amendment; for now *Plyler v. Doe* stands.

▌ Bilingual Education

Another debate that affects the education of immigrant children involves *bilingual education* in schools across the nation. Bilingual education provides academic instruction both in a student's native language and in English. Although bilingual education is not a new idea in the United States, it fell out of favor during World War I. As more and more limited English proficient (LEP) children filled public schools in the mid- and late 1900s, many felt that a return to bilingual education was necessary. Non-English-speaking children were being kept back and labeled "slow learners." Some were even placed in special education classes.

A return to bilingual education began in the 1960s in Miami, Florida.

To assist the children of Spanish-speaking Cuban immigrants, Dade County established a bilingual education program, open to both English- and Spanish-speaking students. The program's goal was for any student who so desired to be bilingual.

In 1974 the Bilingual Education Act required the teaching of LEP students in their native tongue throughout the United States. The goal was to give non-English-speaking children the same academic opportunities as those enjoyed by English-speaking children.

Currently a debate is raging in many parts of the country about the effectiveness of bilingual education. Supporters say that bilingual education preserves the immigrant student's native culture and builds a sense of self-esteem by allowing the child to achieve academically. Opponents say that bilingual education harms immigrant students by hampering their assimilation into American culture. They also say that public

The sign outside this Siler City, North Carolina, kindergarten class reads "Welcome" in Spanish. Nearly half of Siler City's kindergarten students are Hispanic, and many do not speak English.

schools are doing a poor job of educating immigrant children.

In California, home to nearly half the nation's 3 million LEP students, some people have moved to end bilingual education. One plan calls for students to be placed in "English immersion programs" for a year, then transferred to classes in which only English is spoken. Other states, counties, and cities have moved to make English the official language. In many cases such plans would put an end to bilingual education and other bilingual services.

Ellis Island Museum Oral History Project

NAME: Pilar Mendez Bertomeu / Sally Mendez Selles
COUNTRY: Spain
YEAR IMMIGRATED: 1923
AGE: 20 years / 14 years
INTERVIEWER: Paul E. Sigrist Jr.

SIGRIST: Sally, talk to me a little bit about your mother. Tell me what she did when she first got to this country.

SELLES: Oh… I stay home with her. She went to work, you know. I stayed home. They didn't send me to school. I go shopping, she goes shopping, you know, for food, and I go with her, all that.

SIGRIST: So your mother didn't get a job right off the bat.

SELLES: No, no, she didn't get a job.

SIGRIST: Was your mother kind of frightened by it all?

BOTH: No.

SELLES: No.

BERTOMEU: I got a job because there were a lot of people from Spain, girls, and they make me go to there and I got a job right away, and then in sewing….

SIGRIST: So you were… kind of the breadwinner of the family. You were bringing home the paychecks.

BERTOMEU: Oh, yeah. I never take a penny from there.

SIGRIST: And your brother too. He went with you?

SELLES: Yeah. But then after, you know, passed three months, maybe four months, maybe, and I was home. And one day two detectives came home…. And they told me, you know. If Monday she's not in school, $250 fine. And, you know, in those times, $250 was a lot of money. So that's how I went over here to school.

SIGRIST: Sort of forced to, in a way.

SELLES: I don't even know how to put my name, how to write my name.

BERTOMEU: Even me. I'm older than her…. One time they come into the house, and my mother say, "A man was just over here." She say, "You got to go to school in the night." They want you to learn, you know. And you know what my brother say?… He say, "In the night only go the bad girls to school."

SIGRIST: So this is the mentality that we're dealing with. This is how they felt about women getting an education.

SELLES: Right, right.

SIGRIST: Even when he came to this country, your brother is still thinking in these Old World sort of ways.

BERTOMEU: And in Spain he went to school while my father was alive, and he goes in the day to the school....

SIGRIST: Well, so did you eventually go to night class?

BERTOMEU: This don't go on the record.

SIGRIST: Did you go to night classes in Newark? Did you finally?

BERTOMEU: No, because he told me don't go. Only bad girls go to school in the night.

SIGRIST: That's terrible. Well, Sally, tell me about going to school for those two years.

BERTOMEU: So I'm the dope in the family.

SELLES: Monday came, my brother took me to school.

SIGRIST: Did he feel differently about you going to school because you were younger?

SELLES: Well, he feel different because they really forced them to send [me] to school....

BERTOMEU: It's more fair in this country.

SELLES: So I went. I didn't know what they were talking about.

BERTOMEU: Education is best.

SIGRIST: Tell me how you learned English, Sally.

BERTOMEU: Well, she went...

SELLES: I went only two years to school, you know, and I didn't know nothing in Spanish because no numbers, and nothing, almost. And it took me a lot, because they put me in a class with little kids, ABC. [She laughs.]

SIGRIST: How did you feel about that?

SELLES: It was hard. And I didn't feel like staying there, you know, with the little kids. But then I went to the third grade, you know, third or fourth, which I improve a little, you know. They told me, I used to write my name like that, you know. Like this. [She gestures.] I write like this, the way I learn.

SIGRIST: Do you remember when it all made sense to you? Do you remember that moment when suddenly you understood English?

SELLES: Yeah.

SIGRIST: I mean, was there a moment where it just kind of clicked on inside of you?

SELLES: Yeah.

SIGRIST: Do you remember that? Did you help teach your mother English? How did your mother learn, or did she learn?

SELLES: Well, I help her to get the American citizen. That's how she brought the other kids from Spain, see, the American citizen. So I tried to, you know, teach them, teach her.

SIGRIST: Teach your mother.

SELLES: Yeah.

SIGRIST: Was that hard?

SELLES: Oh, yeah, yeah.

SIGRIST: What kinds of things did you have to teach her for her to get her citizenship papers?

SELLES: Everything. If they ask, "What's your name?" … say, and how … many kids you have, when did your husband die, and when you left Spain. Things that they are supposed to ask, you know, all those things.

SIGRIST: Did you have to teach her American history too? Did she have to answer questions about…

SELLES: Yeah, the American flag, about the senators, representatives.

BERTOMEU: Sometimes … she goes [she demonstrates mumbling] and she doesn't open her mouth.

SELLES: I remember when she got the immigrant citizens papers.

The Ellis Island Immigration Museum opened to the public in 1990. The building once housed the Immigration Service.

SIGRIST: Was it hard for her to learn? Because, I mean, she's so much older, of course.

SELLES: Yeah.

SEE ALSO: Assimilation; Charitable Organizations and Mutual Aid Societies; Cultural Pluralism; Language Issues; Prejudice and Discrimination

ELLIS ISLAND HOSPITAL

See **ENTRY PROCEDURES; VOLUME 2:** *ELLIS ISLAND: GATEWAY TO AMERICA*

ELLIS ISLAND NATIONAL MONUMENT

After Ellis Island was closed as an immigration center in 1954, the site was abandoned. Over time the buildings fell into ruin, and thieves stripped the buildings of copper pipes, wiring, and other valuables.

On May 11, 1965, President Lyndon Johnson signed a proclamation recognizing the historic significance of Ellis Island and incorporating it into the Statue of Liberty National Monument. However, nothing was done to restore the site.

As the 1986 *centennial* (100-year) celebration of the Statue of Liberty drew near, interest in Ellis Island grew. A project to repair and restore the main building was begun by the National Park Service and the Statue of Liberty/Ellis Island Foundation. With the generous help of the American people, a restoration effort of unprecedented scale began in 1982. A team of architects and artisans researched and restored Ellis Island's main building to the appearance it had during the years 1918 to 1924.

The Ellis Island National Monument opened to the public in 1990. The centerpiece of the monument is the Ellis Island Immigration Museum, which covers 200,000 square feet within the halls of the main building. More than 30 galleries are filled with artifacts, photographs, and maps telling the story of what happened to the immigrants who passed through its doors. Guided tours, an award-winning film titled *Island of Hope, Island of Tears,* an interactive learning center, an extensive oral history collection, and changing exhibits featuring specific ethnic groups and experiences all chronicle Ellis Island's role in history and give voice to the immigrants themselves.

Outside the museum is the American Immigrant Wall of Honor. The memorial includes 420,000 names submitted by family and friends to honor their immigrant ancestors. It is the most extensive wall of names in the world, and more are always being added.

Ellis Island is one of the country's most-visited sites. The museum is open year-round and is accessible by ferry from New York City and Jersey City, New Jersey.

SEE ALSO: Entry Procedures; Volume 2: *Ellis Island: Gateway to America*

EMPLOYMENT OPPORTUNITIES

See FAMILY AND HOME LIFE

FURTHER READING

Anderson, Kelly. *Immigration.* San Diego: Lucent Books, 1993.

Ashabranner, Brent K. Photos by Jennifer Ashabranner. *Still a Nation of Immigrants.* New York: Cobblehill, 1993.

Backer, Karen. *Immigration: Then & Now.* New York: Scholastic, 1997.

Coan, Peter M. *Ellis Island Interviews: In Their Own Words.* New York: Facts on File.

Collier, C., and J. L. Collier. *American Immigrants, 1840–1900.* Tarrytown, NY: Marshall Cavendish, 1999.

Cozic, Charles. *Illegal Immigration.* San Diego: Greenhaven Press, 1996.

Davies, Wendy. *Closing the Borders.* Austin, TX: Raintree Steck-Vaughn Publishers, 1995.

Freedman, Russell. *Immigrant Kids.* New York: Puffin, 1995.

Hadden, Gerald. *Teenage Refugees from Guatemala Speak Out.* New York: The Rosen Publishing Group, 1997.

Horrell, Sarah. *The History of Emigration from Eastern Europe* (Origins). Danbury: Franklin Watts, 1998.

Jacobs, Nancy R., Mark A. Siegel, and Alison Laudes, eds. *Immigration: Looking for a New Home.* Wylie, TX: Information Plus, 1997.

Jacobs, William Jay. *Ellis Island: New Hope in a New Land.* New York: Atheneum, 1990.

Kawaguchi, Gary, and Miriam Sagan. *Tracing Our Japanese Roots.* Santa Fe: John Muir Publications, 1994.

Kroll, Steven. Illus. by Karen Ritz. *Ellis Island: Doorway to Freedom.* New York: Holiday House, 1995.

Kurelek, William, and Margaret Engelhart. *They Sought a New World: The Story of European Immigration to North America.* Plattsburgh, NY: Tundra Books, 1988.

Ladybird Staff. *Migrations.* New York: Penguin USA, 1997.

Lawlor, Veronica. *I Was Dreaming to Come to America: Memories from the Ellis Island Oral History Project.* New York: Viking Children's Books, 1995.

Leder, Jane M. *The Russian Jewish Experience.* Minneapolis: The Lerner Publishing Group, 1996.

Lee, Kathleen. *Tracing Our Italian Roots* (American Origins). Santa Fe: John Muir Publications, 1993.

Levine, Ellen. Illus. by Wayne Parmenter. *If Your Name Was Changed at Ellis Island.* Scholastic Trade, 1994.

Levine, Herbert M. *Immigration.* Austin, TX: Raintree Steck-Vaughn Publishers, 1998.

Levinson, David, and Melvin Ember, eds. *American Immigrant Cultures: Builders of a Nation.* Vols. I & II. Indianapolis: MacMillan Publishing, 1997.

Morrow, Robert. *Immigration: Blessing or Burden?* Minneapolis: The Lerner Publishing Group, 1997.

Moscinski, Sharon. *Tracing Our Irish Roots* (American Origins). Santa Fe: John Muir Publications, 1993.

Prior, Katherine. *The History of Emigration from Italy* (Origins). Danbury: Franklin Watts, 1998.

Reef, Catherine. *Ellis Island* (Places in American History). Dillon Press, 1991.

Rollyson, Carl. *Teenage Refugees from Eastern Europe Speak Out.* New York: The Rosen Publishing Group, 1997.

Sandler, Martin W., and James Billington. *Immigrants* (A Library of Congress Book). New York: HaperCollins Juvenile Books, 1995.

Schapper, Ladena. *Teenage Refugees from Ethiopia Speak Out.* New York: The Rosen Publishing Group, 1997.

Stein, Richard Conrad. *Ellis Island* (Cornerstones of Freedom). Danbury: Children's Press, 1994.

Steoff, Rebecca, and Ronald Takaki. *Spacious Dreams: The First Wave of Asian Immigration* (The Asian American Experience). Broomall, PA: Chelsea House, 1994.

Strom, Yale. *Quilted Landscapes: Immigrant Youth in the United States.* Simon & Schuster, 1996.

Takaki, Ronald. *Ethnic Islands: The Emergence of Urban Chinese America* (The Asian American Experience). Broomall, PA: Chelsea House, 1994.

Tanner, Helen Hornbeck, Janice Reiff, and John H. Long, eds. *The Settling of North America: The Atlas of the Great Migrations into North America from the Ice Age to the Present.* Indianapolis: MacMillan Publishing, 1996.

Twagilimana, Aimable. *Teenage Refugees from Rwanda Speak Out.* New York: The Rosen Publishing Group, 1997.

Viswanath, Rupa. *Teenage Refugees from India Speak Out.* New York: The Rosen Publishing Group, 1997.

SET INDEX

Text printed on 70# Courtland matte, with Birch embossed endsheets
Printer: World Color Book Services, Taunton, MA.

Covers designed by Smart Graphics, East Haddam, CT; printed on 80# C1S
post-embossed. Cover printer: Mid-City Lithographers, Lake Forest, IL.